HERITAGE SKILLS
For Contemporary Living

SEASONS AT THE PARRIS HOUSE

Elizabeth Miller

Down East Books

CAMDEN, MAINE

Down East Books

Published by Down East Books

An imprint of Globe Pequot

Trade division of The Rowman & Littlefield Publishing
Group, Inc.

4501 Forbes Blvd., Ste. 200

Lanham, MD 20706

www.rowman.com

www.downeastbooks.com

Distributed by NATIONAL BOOK NETWORK

Designed by Lynda Chilton, Chilton Creative

ISBN 978-1-60893-679-3 (paperback)
ISBN 978-1-60893-680-9 (e-book)

♾™ The paper used in this publication meets the minimum
requirements of American National Standard for Information Sciences—Permanence of Paper for Printed Library
Materials, ANSI/NISO Z39.48-1992.

To Bill,
Rob, Tracy, & Oliver,
James & Beth,
Peter,
Paul & Gabi

Courtesy Historic New England

CONTENTS

~~~~~~

546

Heritage Styles for Contemporary Living

INTRODUCTION

What Happens When a Suburban Family Finds a Home in Rural Maine

The week we moved into the Parris House, in March of 2000, we were given a warm, Maine welcome. Some may find that surprising, as Mainers have an undeserved reputation for being aloof or worse to those of us "from away," however that was not my experience here on Paris Hill. One of the older women whose family and ancestors have occupied our National Historic District for over two centuries arrived on the doorstep with pizzas and Coca Cola, having noticed that we had four young sons to feed while we all settled in to a place immediately beloved, but still pretty alien. An elderly woman, who unbeknownst to me at the time was a pillar of the village and larger community, brought us home-baked cookies and welcomed us warmly. More cookies came from a young mother about my age, a woman who would become one of my best friends, and my next-door neighbors invited us to dinner within the week. Some weeks later a welcoming reception was held for me by the other women of the neighborhood. I felt immediately welcomed, and yet . . . I also felt a bit lost.

I was thirty-five years old with a husband and four young sons, ages two to ten at the time. I had been born in the Philadelphia suburbs, grown up in southern New Jersey, earned a degree in Business Administration/Marketing at the University of Delaware, and then eventually lived in both Levittown, Pennsylvania and Pennington, New Jersey. I had worked for a large aerospace corporation along the busy

Route 1 corridor. In other words, I had spent my life living and working in the urban/suburban Mid Atlantic.

Despite this, I had Maine ties. I had summered many years on Little Sebago Lake in Gray with my maternal grandparents. For some of us, Maine gets under our skin and into our very DNA, and from that point on we are destined to return, even if it takes decades. It took me until I was thirty-five, and while the breathtakingly beautiful Maine environment was familiar, the lifestyle was not.

I noticed it immediately. The woman who brought us the pizza and Coke told us about the ancient golden chain tree in front of the house, the one we thought of cutting down because it was introducing carpenter ants to our upstairs. She said that it was on the Maine Registry of Big Trees and that it was the oldest and largest of its kind in the state. She went on to tell us more about the plantings on the property, what was still there and what she remembered from childhood. She also told me to find out about "Pedro," an ex-slave who had lived in our home. I marveled at how casually she demonstrated both her horticultural and historical knowledge. I remember thinking, "I wonder if all of this is true?" But I had a houseful of things to unpack and while I was genuinely interested, the research would have to wait.

Our neighbor across the street had a cow in her back yard, much to the delight of my four young sons. Sometimes they could catch a glimpse of it from their upstairs bedroom windows. Other times they'd just hear it mooing.

When our neighbors invited us to dinner, we learned about how they had restored their nineteenth century home themselves. I saw how quilt making, and rug hooking and braiding, were arts handed down from my neighbor's grandmother to her. Her home was beautifully appointed with pieces made by several generations of the family. Later in the year I watched in awe as she tended her colorful and fragrant New England flower garden, which was spectacular to me, but she seemed to regard as an everyday hobby.

I went to the welcoming reception thrown in my honor down the street, to find that the hostess had chickens in her barn and was the neighborhood source for fresh eggs. I had never eaten eggs that didn't come from a supermarket.

No one kept cows or chickens or bees or any other livestock in the neighborhoods I'd lived in. In fact, some places probably had ordinances prohibiting those things. Paris Hill is a village of relatively small lots. I was not among large farms. The main drag of South Paris was only two and a half miles down the Hill, with McDonald's, Burger King, Dunkin Donuts, and other signs of modern "civilization." The heritage skills I had come to associate with extremely rural areas, large farm parcels, or simply days long gone, were alive and well not only in my new home village, but all over Maine.

I was determined to learn these ways, and I did. And because I was able to, I know you can too. That is what this book is all about.

In 2000 I had no idea that there would be such a resurgence in the practice of heritage skills. People grow gardens and keep bees on urban roof tops. They enjoy fresh eggs from their own backyard chickens. Fiber festivals and open farm days are popular events year-round and farmers' markets are becoming a preferred source for both purchasing and selling fresh, local foods. The term "handmade" has gone from being considered quaint but inferior to mass-produced goods to once again representing skill, craftsmanship, and superior quality. Many people, of all ages, are also taking an interest in genealogy and DNA testing that reveals their geographical lineage, bringing their own personal history into their contemporary lifestyle. As they find out about themselves, they become interested in their local history as well and how they, their family, their homes, and their towns fit into a larger context of community. All of this is occurring with the assistance of technological advances that put more information within our quick and easy reach than at any other time in history, which brings me to my next point.

We need not eschew modern living and technology to practice heritage skills and derive benefit and personal satisfaction from them. It is not necessary to live off the grid. Additionally, you do not need a farm, or even a great deal of land, or, I'd argue, land at all, to incorporate some of these activities into your lifestyle. In this book I will always explain whether a skill or project requires a specific amount of space or type of environment. For example, common sense, good husbandry practices, and local laws may dictate space and location restrictions for keeping live animals, however most projects in this book will not require a specific type of home or yard.

I have taken care to only include projects and recipes that can be done with easily available materials and without extremely specialized skills or overly complicated processes. This does not mean that these projects are so simple as to insult your intelligence or not be valuable. You will learn solid heritage skills and will hopefully conclude, as I did, that nothing is "rocket science," but rather just a matter of instruction and practice. It is also important to note that I have covered each topic according to what works well for us here at the Parris House, often based in the philosophy that keeping things simple is best. In any area of practice, there are multiple ways of doing things. Hopefully these serve as a start for you to find your own best ways.

It took me almost two decades and a meandering path to learn the variety of skills contained in this book. This is because all the while I was also raising children, working in a real estate career, volunteering, and living a generally busy life. I know it's likely that your life is just as filled with activity and you possibly feel short on time. I want this book to be a short-cut for you, an introduction to a wide variety of arts and skills from which you can choose to determine which ones resonate for you and warrant further exploration and inclusion in your life. This book serves as a sampler, season by season, of things to try. It is therefore by no means an exhaustive, expert primer on every topic it covers, but rather a way of introduction into each skill. It is not necessary to do every project in every season, nor is it necessary to work through the book in a single year. It is designed to be a springboard for your individual lifestyle. It is also meant to be a guide that family, friends, parents, grandparents, and children – in whatever combination! – can use to make memories by choosing projects to work on together. Ultimately, knowledge is transferred person to person within community, so please consider using the book as couples, families, or friend and community groups as well.

Inspiration and practices flow from your life context. Your life context includes your experiences, your family, your friends, your work and passions, your town, your state, region, and country. What follows is a bit of context for my life at the Parris House here in Maine. It is the setting for all the projects, images, recipes, and overall philosophy offered in this book, and yet you will find the content adaptable to your own context as well. It explains how my sense of place here influenced my own journey to making and doing, and how my journey is connected to the people who came before me in this centuries-old home and community.

In a larger sense, this book also serves as a gateway to a manner of living that puts us in closer communion with our senses and back into our bodies and the three-dimensional world. As much as I love technology, I know that it often removes me from an in-the-moment awareness of the physical world. Far from being a barrier to the spiritual, the physical and natural world grounds us in an appreciation for both the blessings it contains and the relative brevity of our experience here. When our bodies and minds are focused on something as simple but beautiful as picking an apple, inspecting a frame of bees, smelling an Italian gravy simmering, or pulling wool loops through linen to create art, we are truly immersed in the human experience. These things are of the earth. We are of the earth. I hope the activities in this book will help you to feel connected to our common planet and to our human family, both those living and long gone from us but forever remembered in the love and heritage passed down.

Courtesy Historic New England

ABOUT THE PARRIS HOUSE

In 1973, Paris Hill village became the Paris Hill Historic District, National Register ID 73000243. Its areas of significance were designated as architecture, primarily in the Greek Revival and Federal styles, and politics/government. The Parris House is considered a contributing structure to the district, but all of that seems almost clinical compared to the deeply inspiring history behind this village and this home.

In 1818, the year the Parris House was built, future President Abraham Lincoln was nine years old. His Paris Hill-born and raised running mate, Hannibal Hamlin, was also nine years old. John Adams and Thomas Jefferson were still living. Maine would not become a state for two more years. The village of Paris Hill had sprung up from Revolutionary War veterans' land grants and become the county seat of Oxford County, Maine. According to the best records we can find, the original structure of the Parris House was put up by George Ryerson and then transferred very soon thereafter to Alfred and Eliza Cushman Andrews, who lived here until 1853, when they built a new home closer to village center. They sold the Parris House to Virgil Delphini Parris and his wife, Paris Hill native, Columbia Rawson Parris for $1,100. It is this family's name that has "stuck" all of these years and which I learned upon our family's arrival in 2000.

My neighbor, Edie, was a Rawson family descendant, Columbia Rawson Parris having been the sister of Edie's foremother, Frances Rawson Kimball. It was Edie who showed up on our doorstep first that day we moved in, with pizzas and sodas for all of us and a bright smile on her face as she said, "Welcome to the Parris House!" It was the first

I'd heard its name. She proceeded to tell me about Percival Parris, the last living Parris to inhabit the home, firing off his family's Revolutionary War musket on the village green each Fourth of July when she was a child. She said not to dare cut the golden chain tree, which had been there a century and was the biggest and oldest of its kind in Maine. And then she told me about Pedro Tovookan, the formerly enslaved African who had lived and died there.

To be honest, I took it all with a grain of salt. The real estate broker had mentioned none of this, which I thought odd considering it should have added interest to the home. What I did not know then is that in Maine, where we have some of the oldest houses in the nation, many homes have fascinating and even important histories and to some buyers, and unfortunately some brokers, these stories are too common to note. But then I started hearing more.

My neighbors across the street seemed to know about Pedro Tovookan also, and when I finally took a walk in the cemetery directly behind my new home, I found his grave. I wondered about this. I wondered about all of it. Thus, began what has become a nearly two decade, on again, off again search for who this man really was and what it means to me to be a steward of the Parris House.

One of the first artifacts I found regarding Tovookan was his obituary, in the then Paris Hill based Oxford Democrat, for Friday, April 13th, 1860:

> **Died in this village, Tuesday, Pedro Taocan (sic), a native of Africa. While Honorable V.D. Parris was the Marshal of Maine, a slaver was captured, having left on board but two of the Africans that had composed her cargo. These lads, after acting as witnesses, were taken in charge, one by Mr. Parris, and the other by the Marshal of Massachusetts. The**

family taught Pedro our language, gave him a good education, and have treated him in every respect as one of their number. He has always maintained an affectionate regard for them, devoting himself faithfully to their interests, and refusing to leave them. He had also adopted the name of the family who had befriended him. His funeral was attended Wednesday afternoon, by a large number of our citizens. Few have gone from our midst, whose loss is more generally or sincerely mourned.

Courtesy Parris Hill Historical Society

I was immediately struck by the last sentence. Tovookan had been sincerely beloved, a previously enslaved, free black man in an overwhelmingly white environment in Antebellum New England. It is important to note that the position lines on slavery in the United States were not as neatly drawn as many of us have been led to believe. New England profited mightily from the slave trade and there were many, including Virgil D. Parris himself, who identified as states' rights Democrats. Paris Hill born Hannibal Hamlin, who went on to serve as Abraham Lincoln's first Vice President, espoused a very different philosophy as a member of the newly formed Republican Party and as a supporter of abolition. This, in itself, was intriguing.

There is plenty of evidence that Tovookan was sincerely cared for by his adoptive family. Arabella Rawson Carter was Tovookan's adoptive aunt, sister to Columbia Parris. Her first mention of his illness in her diaries is on March 30, 1860. Please note that Arabella uses Tovookan's slave name, Pedro, the one given him by a Portuguese ship captain and by which he was known to the community on Paris Hill. I use his African name out of respect for his original home and ancestral history.

"Pedro remains unwell. Dr. Brown thinks he has a bilious fever."

Almost every day between this entry and April 8th's, Arabella notes Tovookan's fluctuating condition. However, on April 9th she writes:

"Pedro more unwell, applied mustard bathes, stayed all afternoon and evening."

April 10th brings terrible news:

"Went over to see Pedro. As soon as I conveniently could, found him very feeble but not apparently worse than yesterday. Went home to breakfast and immediately after heard that Pedro was worse, perhaps dying, went directly and found him dead. All of us are filled with sorrow. Mr. Parris and Kimball abroad. Samuel telegraphed for them and told them the sad news."

On April 11th, Arabella writes:

"Pedro is to be buried today, decomposition taking place rapidly. Funeral to take place at half past four this afternoon. Mr. Parris arrived after the people were all assembled. Vivian Chase officiated at the funeral services at the grave after the manner of Methodists. We have passed a solemn day."

It is clear from the primary source material that Tovookan was regarded with affection by his adoptive family and by the community. However, evidence that he was not regarded as fully equal haunts me. The first time I visited Tovookan's grave, which is literally just over the stone cemetery wall, a matter of yards from our gardens, I noticed it was not like those of the other Parris family members. It is smaller, much simpler, off to the side, almost at the very boundary edge of the family cemetery. It says simply:

Pedro Tovookan
A native of Zanzsucbar (sic), Africa
Died April 10th, 1860
AEt. 27

The Parris name is not on the stone, nor is the grave anywhere near the Parris family graves. Perhaps in 1860, the antebellum era of heated disagreement over slavery and the rights of both free and enslaved Africans, in a then politically important village many of whose politicians identified as states' rights Democrats, a more inclusive or embracing burial could not be expected. On the other hand, it is also possible that for Tovookan to have been buried in the family plot at all was an honor that in 1860 might have been denied to others in his situation. We cannot know for sure, however, given the historical context of antebellum New England and his adoptive family's political philosophy, it seems likely that Tovookan would not have enjoyed fully equal status to his white neighbors on Paris Hill. Had he lived to see the Civil War and its aftermath, it is anyone's guess what trajectory his life might have taken.

In 1860, dying of "bilious fever," an ailment that could encompass any number of more well-defined infections and diseases today, would not have been unusual. Yet, although Tovookan suffered a tragically ordinary death, his life had been extraordinary.

An in-depth biography of Pedro Tovookan Parris is beyond the scope of this brief history of the Parris House, so I will point out the most remarkable aspects of his life.

Tovookan was born around 1833 somewhere on the eastern coast of Africa. Around 1843, he was abducted in a nighttime raid by slave traders in which his family was scattered. One of his last recollections of the raid was that of seeing his grandmother screaming in anguish on a rock. He was then led on a weeks-long forced march to Zanzibar, which was an important slave trading hub at the time. We know from this history that he was not a native of Zanzibar, as his gravestone states, but from an area some weeks' travel on foot away.

Courtesy Historic New England

From there, Tovookan was sold to a Portuguese slave trader, who gave him the name "Pedro," and who in turn sold him to a Portuguese Captain Paulo. Tovookan found himself and other enslaved Africans aboard the *Porpoise*, a ship owned by Captain Cyrus Libby of Maine. Some of the crew aboard the Porpoise did not approve of being involved in trafficking slaves and upon the ship's arrival to Rio de Janeiro in 1845, they alerted the U.S. Consul there, George Gordon, of the illegal activity. The ship was impounded, and its captain apprehended and sent back to Maine, via Boston, for trial. It was there that Tovookan first met Virgil D. Parris, who was the United States Marshal for Maine and assisting in the prosecution.

Tovookan served as a witness in the trial, and when it was completed, was taken in permanently by the Parris family who, at the time, lived in Portland, Maine. He may well have gotten to know the free black community in Portland and made friends there, prior to moving to the Parris House in 1853.

American Consul to Brazil at the time of the trial, George Gordon ran unsuccessfully for Governor of Massachusetts in 1856 and asked Tovookan to speak on behalf of his campaign, which he did. Tovookan also became an artist, with one of his extant watercolor works, a panorama of his journey from Rio de Janeiro to Paris, Maine, now in the possession of Historic New England. There are also written accounts of him serving oysters in a local tavern. Percival Parris, a boy at the time of Tovookan's death, recalled Tovookan teaching him African songs in his native language.

In this briefest account of his life, I am hoping to convey that Tovookan was manifestly brave, personally successful, and resilient. Given that his early life was marked by the most abject cruelty, including having been branded on the chest, and that it is doubtful, in antebellum America, that he would

1 Minnie Carter
2 Mrs J.R. Kimball
3 Ald Jason?
4 Mrs Ingraham
5 P.J. PARRIS
6 Molly Davies
7 DOROTHEA CARTER
8 JULIA CARTER
9 unknown
10 Helen PARRIS
11 COLUMBIA PARRIS
12 Mrs FRANNIE CARTER
13 Polly Davies

Courtesy Historic New England

ever be permitted an equal place in society, Tovookan's life of achievement is inspiring. It is for this reason that when I am asked about the history of the Parris House, I start with Tovookan as its most prominent prior resident, the individual whose story I am most compelled to share with the world. From there I do speak also about Virgil D. Parris, Congressman, U.S. Marshal for Maine, and acting Governor of Maine, and his wife Columbia, for they were the ones who found it in their hearts to bring Tovookan into their family.

Tovookan told Percival J. Parris, his young adoptive brother, that his African name meant, "to run away" and that it had been given him because of his "noncombative disposition." Perhaps Tovookan was gentle and non-confrontational, but he also clearly possessed a rare strength of character. He is very much alive to us here at the Parris House, where his spirit and story continue to inspire.

SPRING

An Auspicious Beginning

Spring gets a slow start here in Western Maine. Living through spring in Maine is an exercise in patience, expectation, hope, and faith. The spring solstice, as you know, happens right around March 21st of every year, but here in Maine spring is rarely in evidence on that date. In fact, there is usually plenty of snowpack left if not outright snowstorms roaring in, sometimes well into April. Coming from a more temperate climate, I had to get used to this in my initial years here. But it reinforced what I already know about myself: I am not naturally patient, and I sometimes lose faith.

Two of my sons were born in March around the spring solstice, one on the 21st and one on the 26th. They were born in the temperate Mid Atlantic region of the United States and I clearly remember taking them out as newborns in strollers with warmish sunshine on our faces and bulbs popping up all around our suburban neighborhood. I think of that every year in March still, often while watching horizontally blowing snow outside my windows here in Maine. But Maine has taught me, on a thousand different occasions, that patience and faith here are almost always rewarded. Not without some trial, however.

Maine has one more trick up its sleeve before the spring we all envision finally arrives. That trick is mud season. You may know the old joke. There are five seasons in Maine: spring, summer, fall, winter, and mud. It's not really a joke.

It's very real. I'd argue there are six and include blackfly season also.

My area of Maine gets several feet of snow each winter. When all that melts, it must go somewhere. It melts off the mountain tops and high ground and pours down into the rivers, streams, and lower lands. There are spring floods, what our ancestors called "freshets," both from the melting snow and ice and, in some cases, from ice jams on the bigger rivers. What the water bodies can not hold, the land tries, and often fails, to absorb. Here at the Parris House, we have an underground spring that bubbles to the surface this time of year and runs down the yard and under the barn, much to our dismay as we know this cannot be good for the barn foundation. All of this runaway water results in mud, and lots of it.

I tell would-be visitors and tourists that mud season is the only time Maine could possibly be characterized as ugly. The trees are still bare, what's left of the snowpack is dirty with road salt, sand, and dirt, and anything that littered the ground before the first good snow is reemerging all the worse for wear. The landscape is still barren but without the majestic, glittering drape of snow and ice. Instead it looks like a wet, dirty puppy just rescued from an unfortunate fall into the farm pond. You will get mud everywhere, including in the house despite your best efforts. There may be shoes lined up on the doorstep or in your mud room, but the mud is still getting into the house…somehow. As in life, though, when everything seems just about at its ugliest, an eye trained by patience and inspired by hope can see the signs of positive change coming.

When all seems gray during a Maine spring, look for the emergence of the earliest plants, both domesticated and wild. In many gardens, snow drops appear first, followed by the little green shoots that will become daffodils. In the wild, fiddlehead ferns are among the first plants to appear along with early evidence of trillium. On the warmest days, the long dormant beehives will come to life as the bees venture out for "cleansing flights." If you see little, round yellow dots on your car windshield you might just have been visited by some bees doing the most basic of bee business on your car. The ice on the lakes will start to thin and break up near the shorelines, creating mosaics of broken ice that look like shards of glass. Sunrise will come earlier, and you may be awakened by bird-song for the first time in months. By the time you notice the first blackfly, Spring has taken hold and the time is right to start your own plans for Maine's growing season.

Springtime in Maine is a time for indoor work and cleaning when the weather is inclement and the preparation for the growing and gardening season when the sun shines. The weather is also extremely unpredictable during the spring, so what follows is a wide variety of indoor and outdoor activities to keep you busy no matter what Mother Nature is dishing out.

Spring Homesteading

Evaluating for Spring Repairs

Early springtime in Maine is revealing. The time between the end of the snow season and the reemergence of plant life makes the landscape seem a bit bleak and naked. It is the same with buildings and structures on your homestead. There is no better time of year than this to bluntly assess any damage winter has wrought or any neglected corner normally hidden by lush foliage.

To help you with this, I have created the following checklist, by no means exhaustive, for you to use in early spring to evaluate any repairs that may be needed before the snow flies again. Feel free to add your own items as may apply to your homestead. I recommend that you put your checklist on to a hard clipboard and just spend an hour or so walking around your property, making notes, prioritizing, and thinking about scheduling repairs. While this can possibly feel a little overwhelming, I find that if I have a worksheet to refer back to, the tasks are more manageable to plan and execute than if I try to go by memory or worse, go to use something forgetting it had a problem.

If you do your walk around and find that your to-do list is short or nonexistent, congratulations! This means that you are doing an excellent job of meticulously maintaining your homestead. For most of us, however, shortages of time, funds, or just life getting in the way mean that springtime is fix-it time.

SPRING CHECK LIST

- ☐ Beekeeping: Hives, tools, equipment, clothing
- ☐ Chipped & Worn Paint
- ☐ Compost Bin and Composter
- ☐ Docks or piers
- ☐ Doors, Latches, Locks; Windows & Screens
- ☐ Fences
- ☐ Garden Tools
- ☐ Hoses, Sprinklers, Water Supply
- ☐ Ladders and Staging
- ☐ Livestock Waste
- ☐ Organic Debris (leaves, brush, pine needles)
- ☐ Outdoor Furniture
- ☐ Outdoor Steps, Rails, & Decks
- ☐ Perennial Bushes and Trees
- ☐ Placing Cages, Trellises, & Raised Beds
- ☐ Roofs and Shutters
- ☐ Security of Coops and Feed Storage
- ☐ Storm Windows & Screens
- ☐ Tractors, Mowers, & Other Equipment
- ☐ Damaged or Fallen Trees
- ☐ Uncovering Plants
- ☐ Gutters and Water Drainage

Starting Seeds

About six to eight weeks prior to planting your outdoor garden, depending on the plant, you will want to start any seeds for plants that either are not sown directly in the ground or plants that you don't intend to buy as seedlings from a greenhouse later.

You will need:
- Seeds (make sure they are the kind that are best sown indoors)
- Growing medium/seed starter
- Growing trays, including drainage tray, divided growing tray, and clear plastic lid
- Drinking Straw
- Measuring cup
- Grow lights (optional depending on where you locate your trays)
- Small notebook, stickers, pencil or pen

Starting seeds is a very easy, straightforward activity and one that is particularly fun to do with children. The sense of satisfaction kids get from watching seeds sprout, grow, and eventually become a source of food later in the year can provide lessons transferable to many other aspects of their lives. Honestly, the same benefits apply to adults.

Here at the Parris House we have started seeds in two locations. Most recently we started them right on the center island in the kitchen because it has great natural light and also overhead artificial lighting that works well for the plants. However, this is an option that requires the devotion of precious counter space for a significant period of time. Many people don't want to or simply can't do that. Our other growing area has been in our basement, on a table made from

two sawhorses and a sheet of plywood, with grow lights hung above. If neither a kitchen counter nor a basement is available, no worries. Just put your seedlings on a solid base in a relatively sunny and warm or well-lit area of your home, protected from interference from pets and out of the way of your high traffic zones.

After a lot of experimentation, we like the three-part seed starter trays that include a water catching tray in the bottom and a clear plastic lid to retain heat and moisture. These trays are a little more expensive than some other options, but we regard them as labor saving during a season when we are already very busy. The bottom trays catch the excess water, providing additional moisture in the seedlings' atmosphere rather than just evaporating off because of the sealed tops. If whoever's in charge of monitoring the seedlings forgets for a day or so, this arrangement will usually not dry out too quickly. It does have to be monitored for over-watering, but we have never had a problem with seeds rotting, molding, or failing to germinate from too much moisture using this method.

We also like these trays because they are reusable for many years if care is taken not to break or damage them. We are not fans of plastic at the Parris House, especially single use plastics, so when we do use it for something, we try to make sure it's going to be used many times for a long time.

Check the instructions on your seed packets for whether or not they are to be started indoors in the spring or sown directly into your garden once the soil warms later and after the last frost. Seeds commonly started indoors are tomatoes, peppers, lettuce, kale, eggplants, and many cruciferous vegetables. If these seedlings grow to be strong, they take very nicely to transplanting because their root systems are not overly sensitive to that process. Vegetables that are commonly sown directly into the ground are pumpkins, squash, melons, peas, corn, and beans. While all of these have relatively large seeds, there are also tiny seed vegetables that also do better with direct sowing, for example, radishes, carrots, and parsnips. The bottom line is to just read your seed packets carefully and follow your seed supplier's instructions.

Use fresh seed starting medium for your plants each year, meaning, do not reuse the medium from last year's trays. This is because your seedlings are going to use the nutrients in it to grow and starting medium that has already grown other seedlings may be partially depleted. You usually take a lot of medium with the seedlings when you transplant them into the garden later, but just in case you have some left in trays from a previous year, scatter that on to your garden and start with fresh.

I use a 2-cup measuring cup to have a little more control when filling my seed trays with growing medium. It's easier and neater than pouring it directly from the bag, especially if the bag is large. Fill your seed trays about ¾ full with it to prepare them for seed sowing. Slightly dampen the medium using your measuring cup and gently pouring just a little water into each of the divided seed containers.

Decide which trays are going to hold which seeds and then create a labeling system and a diagram for each one. In the example shown, I just used a simple numbering system and then drew a corresponding grid on to pieces of paper for each tray. This is particularly important if you are new to

gardening and cannot readily identify seedlings on sight. If this is the case for you, do not feel at all bad about it! When I first started gardening, I labeled my rows meticulously and then was baffled when some of my row markers went missing. My next thought was, "Well, I guess I'll just wait and see what kind of vegetable comes off of this plant."

When you have your trays mapped out, it's time to finally plant the seeds. I have found that a straw works well for punching out the small space in the growing medium needed to hold the seeds and also helps control the depth at which the seeds are planted. Your seed packs will come with directions for planting depth and how many to plant in a single tray section. Some of these will likely later be thinned out, keeping the strongest and discarding the weakest of the seedlings, but often plants are started with multiple seeds per tray section. Instructions for thinning your seedlings will also be on your seed packets.

Once you've punched out the holes and planted your seeds, cover them lightly with your growing medium. You will need to water them again but do so very gently so that you don't flood the seeds up and out of the trays. Don't let the trays get excessively wet. Put the clear plastic lids on to retain the moisture and heat, then place your trays in a warm location for germination. You can use the top of the refrigerator or near the stove, but you can also have a gentle heat source, like a small space heater if you are using a basement or bedroom area for the seedlings. Make sure they get at least twelve to fourteen hours of light, either naturally or via grow lights.

Your plants will germinate in around five to fifteen days, depending on what they are. Often your seed packets will give an estimated germination time. Once they've sprouted and especially once they are tall enough to touch the tray lid, you can take and keep the clear plastic lid off.

Remember that they will dry out faster with the lid removed, so be vigilant about keeping the soil moist and paying attention to whether or not the plants are wilting at all. If you have your trays near a window or other light source coming from the side, be sure to turn the trays regularly if you find the plants always growing in the same direction.

From this point, keep your seedlings moist and with good light, thinning them per the instructions for each plant. If the plants seem to be getting too large for your trays, you may replant them into larger starter containers also filled with growing medium.

About two weeks before you plan to transplant them into the garden, put the trays outside for an increasing amount of time each day to get them acclimated to the outdoors, although do not expose them to temperatures that are below their hardiness range. This is called "hardening off" the plants so that they will not be shocked and wither upon transplanting.

Of course, the alternative to this entire process is purchasing seedlings later that will be ready to plant when you bring them home. This is more expensive and does not afford you the satisfaction of watching the plants' development from seed. Additionally, you will have many more varieties, including heirloom, to choose from when you are purchasing seeds vs buying seedlings from a greenhouse, even a fairly comprehensive greenhouse. At the Parris House we have done both. Some years we start seeds from scratch and other years, often based on our schedules, we purchase seedlings. In the years that we have purchased seedlings we've missed the ritual of poring over seed catalogs, selecting new varieties to try out that season, and watching them grow, however, our garden bounty has been about equal. The goal of any garden is to produce healthy, nutritious food, and either method will meet that goal!

Preparing Raised Beds

At the Parris House, we have always kept this simple. We started with four 8' x 8' x 6" raised beds some years ago after I found myself spending way more time than I'd like weeding our large garden that was sown directly in the ground. Recently, we added two larger, deeper ones, 10' x 10' x 8", for a total of six. We surround our raised bed area with a solar powered electric deer fence and that has been extremely effective in keeping covert nibblers out of the garden.

There are as many ways to do this as there are gardeners, so what follows is our self-taught method which has yielded a tremendous amount of produce over the years with relatively low maintenance both in terms of the beds themselves and time spent weeding

Siting Your Raised Beds

First, determine where to site your raised beds. The following criteria are what I consider most important:

- Sunshine – Pick a spot that is either full sun or near to it for most of the day. Most vegetables grow best under these conditions and here in northern New England where it's not uncommon for the weather to be chilly morning and night even into July, it helps keep the soil and plants warm, especially in the early and late growing season.

- Drainage – The area should be well drained. You do not want to site your beds where water runs down and/or pools. Not only do you not want your plants to be overwatered, but in some locations, runoff from other areas may contain contaminants.
- Access to irrigation – Your raised beds should be in a location that is easy for you to water. The closer to the source of your water, like an outdoor spigot, the better, especially if you are going to run an irrigation system of some kind.
- Convenience – The closer your garden is to your kitchen door and your tool storage area, the happier you'll be. This is not always possible, and the other criteria should come first.

You may find, after considering all of the criteria, that your "best" spot is smack dab in the middle of your suburban lawn or in front of your urban townhouse. Here in Maine it is not at all out of the question to see "food gardens" on the front lawns of urban and suburban properties around Portland, but each location is different and certainly if your property is part of a homeowners association, siting will depend on what is permitted. This is where compromises may be necessary. Just find the sunniest, flattest, best drained, and most convenient spot on your particular property.

At the Parris House, we have achieved a pretty good location with half of these criteria. The nice, high flat spot on our property that provided enough space for everything I wanted to grow is not that close to the house and barn, so one of my compromises is getting more of my Fitbit steps in every day during the gardening season. A partial solution to this would be to build a garden shed right next to the raised bed area to hold all of our tools instead of our trekking them back

and forth to the barn. This is illustrative of the fact that most simple problems either have simple common-sense solutions or can be lived with.

The other compromise we had to make was running a fairly long irrigation line from the outdoor water source on the house to the garden area. We literally buried a hose all the way from the house to the garden, having it come up just at the electric fence line and attach to a variety of waterers we have for each garden bed section. Installing this, plus the fence, makes for one day at the beginning of the season and one at the end "garden set up" or "garden break down" day, however, we have found it to be worthwhile. The rest of our particular property is either sloping, shaded, or otherwise unsuitable for the garden.

How Big, How Many?

The size and number of your raised beds is really up to you. How much space do you want to devote to your garden? How much food do you want to be able to produce? How many hours a week do you want to devote to the maintenance of the garden and, during harvesting times, picking and possibly preserving your bounty? I think it is often a good idea to start small, with perhaps only one or two raised beds with your priority plants and then build from there one year at a time.

What Kind of Raised Beds?

Again, this is personal preference. I'll be describing our raised beds, but they are by no means the only way to build them or the only type to have. I know a family who used large sliced circles of plastic drainage pipe as raised bed structures, so your own creativity can be your guide as long as you consider the following.

CONTAMINANTS – You do not want anything in your raised bed structure that could possibly leach contaminants or toxins into your soil and therefore into your food. This means that if you purchase or build with wood, it should not be pressure treated. Yes, this means that your wooden raised beds may need to be repaired or replaced more frequently, but one of the advantages of growing your own food is that you can at least partially control how safe and wholesome it is. The same applies to using large tractor tires as raised beds, as I have sometimes seen. This can be an ok folksy application for flower beds if that's your style, but I would not want to grow food in rubber tires that could possibly leach anything undesirable into the soil as they inevitably degrade.

BLACK PLASTIC/LANDSCAPING CLOTH – Putting this in the bottom of your beds is personal preference. There are pros and cons and you have to decide what your goals are. Some of my beds are lined with landscaping cloth at the bottom and some are not. In theory, lining the bottom of the bed with a barrier helps keep weeds from coming up, however, I have found that if I use quality soil and compost for the beds and good, seedless straw mulch in between rows during the gardening season, my weeding is minimal in all of the beds. Additionally, if your beds are not that deep, adding a barrier to the bottom may preclude growing long root vegetables like carrots and parsnips. My first beds were only 6 inches deep and lined with landscaping cloth (live and learn). This influenced what I planted in them.

COST – Almost everything we do at the Parris House is evaluated in part on cost. Simply put, we're pretty thrifty. Think about how much you can afford to spend to start your raised bed garden. If money is no object, you can buy extremely nice, premade wood or stainless-steel raised bed structures, all of the soil and compost to fill them, and even create stone or chipped wood walkways between them to keep mowing/string trimming/maintenance at a minimum. Many people starting out, however, are not able to spend a lot of extra money on a garden and I think the way we have set ours up is doable for most.

Simple Wooden Raised Beds à la The Parris House

YOU WILL NEED:
- Four 2" x 8" x 10' pieces of non-pressure treated lumber, four per bed
- Wood screws, three per corner, at least 3 inches long
- Power drill or hand drill
- Pencil for marking screw holes
- Screwdriver
- Level
- Landscaping cloth (optional), enough to cover the bottom of each bed
- Shovel
- Loam/compost mixture

Lay your landscaping cloth, if using it, down in the area you are planning for your raised bed and cut it just a couple of inches larger than the square box you intend to make.

Lay your lumber for the raised bed out in a square in the location where you want it, on top of the landscaping cloth, if using.

Position the lumber sides up against one another at the corners, creating the rough "box" shape to further refine the positioning of the raised bed. This is the time to see if the bed will lie relatively level. Use your level on top of the lumber pieces to determine this. If the bed will not lay level on your location (and often it won't, even if you've chosen the flattest area you could), work the soil under the sides to make adjustments until you have a relatively flat and even base for the raised bed "frame." This does not have to be perfect, but the beds just have to lay flat enough so that they are not twisting once assembled and so that they are less likely to heave over the winter.

Mark where your screw holes will be for putting the bed together. Match up and pre-drill the screw holes for the corners. Screw the corners together, three screws per corner, to create the box. Make any adjustments you have to, moving the box slightly, shimming low spots beneath it or digging out high spots, to make it lay level in its place. If using landscaping cloth, it should stick out about an inch or so all around the underside of the box, with the weight of the box holding it in place.

If this seems impossibly simple, it's because it is.

Fill the boxes to the top with your loam/compost mixture and you are ready to plant. I recommend filling the boxes all the way to the top at this point because the soil will settle over the course of the season and you may as well start with the boxes completely full. You will also have some soil loss as you weed and as you harvest your vegetables, so just fill the boxes at the outset.

Some Notes on Raised Bed Soil

Back when we were gardening right in the ground at the Parris House, our soil was quite nice. We had dark, rich soil with good nutrients in it, but it was also harder to control. One of the best things about raised bed gardening is that you can control the quality of the soil in the beds more easily than if you have to till compost, nutrients, or correctors in to an in-ground garden.

The first year we had our raised beds, we purchased the soil from a local gardening/landscaping company who recommended a loam/compost mix for vegetable gardens. We took our son's old Ford Ranger to their location, had them fill the pickup bed with the mix, took it home, and shoveled it into the raised garden beds, however, many garden centers will deliver for a small fee.

That's not the end of the story for your raised bed soil, however. As you grow different vegetables in your raised beds, you will be using up some of the nutrients in the soil. There are some good practices to make sure that the soil in your raised beds does not become nutrient depleted.

- Top off the beds every year — We get just enough new soil/compost mix every year to top off the beds and work it as much as possible through the previous year's soil.
- Rotate your "crops" — We never grow the same vegetables in the same bed in consecutive years.
- Use compost — If you are composting, you can add your mature compost (it should look like rich, brown, crumbly earth) to your raised beds and work it in to the soil.
- Test your soil and make additions as needed — The most fool-proof thing to do is send a soil sample to your local cooperative extension for testing. You will receive back a soil profile and recommendations for what to add to it for optimal soil conditions.

Now Just Keep the Critters Out

I have so many gardening disaster stories from my earliest days trying to grow food, most of which involve the wildlife getting more food out of our garden than we did. This is not because we are in a rural location. When we lived in suburban New Jersey, we often had deer clipping off our tulip flowers and eating the English Ivy directly beneath our living room window, so do not believe for a moment that urban/suburban gardeners are exempt from critters with the munchies.

Here in Maine, prior to our finding our way to the right solution, our tender plants through fully ripened vegetables were eaten mostly by deer, groundhogs, and raccoons… that we know of. Also prior to finding our solution, we tried hanging tin pie plates around the garden, a non-electrified barrier, peeing around the garden (truly, I don't want to elaborate too much on this), and just plain eternal vigilance. None of that worked. In fact, I can tell you with great confidence that raccoons know the precise moment when fresh corn ripens and will usually steal the ears and destroy the plants twenty-four to forty-eight hours before you'd planned to harvest them.

Notwithstanding the fact that one of the most accomplished gardeners on Paris Hill does not use a single barrier in his garden, instead seeming to have supernatural beings watching over it, I'm a total believer in low-power electric fences.

I know. This is not a thrifty solution. A solar powered electric critter fence large enough to contain your raised bed garden can be purchased at your local garden, home, or farm supply center and it's not particularly cheap, but in our case, it's been the unfailing solution to losing our harvest. If taken down in the fall and stored indoors over the winter, the fence will last you many years. We have had to replace the solar-charged battery about every two to three years in ours, but other than that it has remained reliable and effective. While I do not recommend touching your electric fence when it is on, ours is gentle enough to humans that you can touch it without harm or even serious discomfort. Most common garden robbers, however, are adequately deterred. Of course, make sure that if you are purchasing a fence for your garden that yours is also gentle enough to be a non-hazard to humans and pets, and especially to children.

Ordering and Installing Bees

Ordering Nucs or Packages—Why We Prefer Packages

Ideally, you will have ordered your nucleus hives (nucs) or packages well before spring. It is important to be in touch with your local bee farms and suppliers to find out what the ordering deadlines and subsequent pick-up dates are. While it is also possible to get an established hive from another beekeeper or take someone's unwanted swarm later in the season, we recommend getting nucs or packages from a reputable supplier for several reasons.

Your local bee farms are either raising their starter colonies themselves or they are getting them from an established wholesale supplier. Known care and expertise have been involved in raising the colonies, and in most cases, there is a limited guarantee and replacement policy for the bees, particularly for the queen that comes with them. Additionally, you will have experts on hand to answer questions and offer solutions, especially through your first challenging seasons as a beekeeper.

Most importantly, if you take someone's established hive, or even a cast-off swarm, there is no way to know what may be with it besides bees. Bees are vulnerable to a variety of diseases and parasites, some easily treated but at least one, American foulbrood, so serious that the only recourse is to burn the hive and its occupants to ash. While American foulbrood is rare, I cannot imagine a more traumatic introduction to beekeeping than discovering it or even some lesser illness afflicting your colony. The objective with introductory beekeeping is to have as encouraging an experience as possible so that the typical and inevitable curveballs inherent in the activity remain manageable.

We prefer packages to nucleus hives. Let's talk a little bit about the difference. Nucleus hives are akin to little miniature beehives and include a queen, a sufficient number of bees to care for her and start the colony, and several already wax drawn frames all ready to pop right into your waiting hive set up. A package of bees, on the other hand, is a ventilated box of bees, about three pounds, a queen still in her queen cage inside the box, and a little can of feed, also in the box. There are no frames in the package. Your new bees will have to draw out their own wax from scratch upon installation into your hives, assuming you are starting with new equipment.

When I was a student in my very first beekeeping class I thought, "Why wouldn't I go with a nuc? It sounds so much easier for me and for the bees." I think for the beginner beekeeper, though, packages have several advantages, the most important being that you will watch your bees establish their home from the very first day. You will see them accept (hopefully!) their new queen, draw wax honeycomb over previously empty frames, start to fill that honeycomb with pollen and nectar, see the first brood come in to being, from egg to larvae to emergent bee, and more. I don't believe there is any substitute for watching this process and while nucs are still very nascent colonies, the learning opportunities with packages are greater.

An important rule of thumb also is: always start with at least two hives. Again, as a fledgling beekeeping student, I didn't really get why this was so important. I just knew that all of my teachers and mentors were telling me it was so and that it was mostly because I would learn more by comparing two hives during my first season. Honestly, I questioned it. I didn't really want to spend the money for two of everything, which brings me to a little side point . . .

Beekeeping is not a cheap hobby. No, no, no, no, no. If

you go into small scale beekeeping with the notion that selling honey and wax products will cover your expenses, you will be disappointed. With chicken keeping it is possible, although not always the case, that egg sales will cover your feed and other chicken related expenses. This is particularly true if you are in an area where farm fresh eggs can bring a premium price. Beekeeping is not like that AT ALL. The equipment is expensive, the necessary protective clothing is expensive, treatments for mites or other problems are expensive, and the bees themselves, nucs or packages, are expensive to purchase (which is why experienced beekeepers love to split hives and catch swarms to add to their apiary). The first season you may not get honey to extract at all by the time you set aside enough to leave on your hives for overwintering. These are not the only factors. Hobby scale beekeeping must be done out of love, fascination, and that first (and continuing) taste of honey you and they worked for together. If you do break even in the first couple of years, consider that a rare and happy achievement.

Heritage Skills for Contemporary Living

Returning to the suggestion of starting with two hives, all of the experts are correct. I learned so much from having two hives my first season that I am now as enthusiastic about making that recommendation as everyone else. In addition to the learning opportunities from having two hives in direct comparison, it also provides a little insurance should one hive start to struggle. There are times when adding a frame of brood from a strong hive to a weak one can make a material contribution to the weak hive's very survival. Having a second hive can sometimes be that source, right there in your own bee yard.

Preparing Your Hives

We use Langstroth hives at the Parris House. Langstroth hives are very common in the United States and are made up of a series of boxes with vertically hanging frames in them, a bottom board, an inner cover, and an outer cover. These hives have two entrances, one along the bottom board and a smaller one at the top of the hive under the outer cover. This creates a flow of ventilation through the hive and more than one entry/exit point for the bees.

There are a variety of different hive styles in use in America and all over the world. A discussion of the pros and cons of each of these is beyond the scope of this book, which is primarily written for beginners. In beekeeping you will find many different opinions on every aspect of the art, and you will also find that beekeepers can be very passionate about their own beekeeping choices. Our choice of Langstroth hives is because we learned from teachers and mentors using them, they are easy to purchase or build yourself, and, a factor in our choice to continue using them, our bees have thrived in them.

Two common sizes are available in Langstroth hive set ups. Most commonly, we see what are called "ten frame

deeps" for the most basic part of the hive, the brood box. This means that these boxes, or hive bodies as they're called, are about 9.5 inches deep and hold ten wax frames. Please be aware that the specific dimensions of hive bodies and equipment can vary slightly from maker to maker. These deep hive bodies have the advantage of holding more bees and brood in one box, however, once completely drawn and filled with brood, bees, and maybe some honey, they can become very heavy, weighing as much as 70 pounds. Most often beekeepers will use deep boxes for the brood area and use smaller, medium "super" boxes above for honey storage. This keeps the honey boxes a bit lighter than if deep boxes were used for this purpose.

When I started beekeeping, I was doing it alone. My husband, at that time, had not overcome his aversion to stinging insects and I was on my own. For this reason, I started the Parris House apiary with the other common box size, eight frame mediums. Eight frame mediums hold, as you might have guessed, eight frames each and are 6.5 inches deep. This significantly reduces the weight of the box when full. An eight-frame medium box full of honey weighs about 40 to 50 pounds. Still not light, but much more manageable than the larger deep. You need two of these boxes to hold the brood in an average hive, however, vs one ten frame deep.

So, you have options in deciding what size boxes to purchase, and for each hive you will also have the appropriate size and number of frames, a bottom board, inner cover, and outer cover.

Ultimately, you need a set up that will accommodate the initial package of bees and then their initial growth period as they draw comb, start raising brood, and expand their population. Your set up should also match your ability to heft the boxes around when full. I highly recommend you seek the advice of a mentor and/or your beekeeping supply shop when choosing.

Other choices you will have are whether to purchase your hives unassembled or assembled, and if assembled, unpainted or painted. Obviously, the most labor intensive, but most economical way to purchase is unassembled/unpainted. Assembling hives from their components is not difficult, but it is time consuming, so if you choose to purchase your equipment this way, just budget an evening or two to build them. If you purchase your hives assembled but unpainted, you'll have to paint the exteriors of all of the boxes, the bottom board, and the outer cover with an exterior latex paint. Buying an assembled, painted hive is the ready-to-go option.

Our first hives were purchased unassembled. We took the time to understand how they were constructed and build them ourselves, including assembling all of the frames. Since that time, we have often purchased them assembled and sometimes even already painted. I do want to remind you that in spite of the inconvenience, unpainted hive parts give you the opportunity to decorate your hives in any way you wish. I painted our original hive boxes purple with bright yellow stencils as décor and as a way for us to distinguish our hives and name them. Our first two colonies were named "Hippy Dippy" and "Fleur de Lis" based on the way I had stenciled them. This is a fun "extra" and if this is important to you, leave yourself time to do the custom painting.

Preparing Your Bee Yard

There are a variety of considerations when preparing a bee yard, or apiary, but among the most important are: sun exposure, wind break, predator evasion, water source, forage source, convenience, space to work the hives, and platform height. Let's take these one at a time.

SUN EXPOSURE: Here in Maine, our climate is relatively cold. We do not have to worry a lot about our bees overheating, but we do have to worry about their ability to stay warm when the weather is at its coldest. Therefore, it's good to site your hives where they are going to get a good amount of direct sunlight every day. We paint our hives colors that lean dark as well so that they will absorb more sunlight rather than deflecting it and hopefully raise the temperature of the hive that much more.

WIND BREAK: This consideration is also related to keeping the hives warm enough. Our apiary is behind our barn in an area that normally receives relentless northwest winds, especially in fall and winter. We have erected a solid PVC wind break directly behind the hives to stop the wind from reaching them from that direction. You may use any kind of fencing or even a very strong tarp, or you may site your hives in a way relative to a building that provides a wind break.

PREDATOR EVASION: Some predators to be avoided are mice, voles, skunks, racoons, but most devastating of all, bears. You will have a good sense of whether or not bears could be a threat where you live, but if they are, consider an electric bear fence for your hives. This may sound drastic, but hives attacked by bears get completely destroyed. The boxes are scattered and broken in a way that looks as though someone detonated an explosive inside the hive. Contrary to bear and bee themed cartoons, and Winnie the Pooh's stated obsession with honey, bears are often after the brood more than they're after the sweet stuff. This is because bee brood is an excellent protein source for hungry bears. If you do opt for an electric bear fence, understand that these are more powerful than the light electric fence I recommend for your garden and can pose a real hazard to humans. For the

smaller predators, good conventional fencing and, season-
ally, mouse guards on the hives, can keep them at bay. My
husband likes to keep the hives strapped closed and to their
base using nylon strapping. This is possibly a "belts and sus-
penders" precaution, but it also doesn't hurt.

WATER SOURCE: Bees forage in approximately a three-mile
radius. A nearby pond, like we have, is ideal for an apiary,
however, if you do not have this, it is perfectly fine to provide
an artificial water source for your bees. If using a shallow
container, like a large pan, fill the bottom with rocks or something else that the bees can get a "perch" on. Likewise, if it's a
bucket, put a few things floating in it that they can use. Do not
have the source too close to the hive as it's a bit harder for the
bees to communicate immediate proximity. Have it more like
seventy-five to one hundred and fifty feet from the hive. If you
happen to have a bee garden or just a regular flower garden
nearby, putting the water source there might work well since
the bees will be attracted to the flowers in any case.

FORAGE SOURCE: As noted above, bees will forage in a
three-mile radius, and can even forage up to five miles if
they have to, although at that range the ratio of the energy
they expend relative to what they take in can be unfavorable.
Bees are very efficient at finding pollen, nectar, and water.
At the Parris House we have a large open field next to the
house which is filled with wildflowers from late spring to
mid-summer, after which it goes into a dearth until the late
summer/early fall flow. This is an excellent source of forage
for our bees, but I know they are also in the gardens of our
neighbors, on the flowers at the historical society half a mile
away, and beyond. The fact that bees are kept in cities on
urban rooftops suggests that they are extremely resourceful in finding forage in a variety of seemingly inhospitable

settings, although honey production in some urban areas has been reported as lower than in rural settings.

When you become a beekeeper, you will notice yourself becoming more aware than ever before of the pollen and bloom cycles in your local environment. Learn about which plants make particularly good forage for your bees and, unless they are horribly invasive (bamboo and Japanese knotweed come to mind – do not plant!), consider planting that on your property. If that is not realistic, be aware of where those plants exist in your immediate two-mile radius or so. Once you are familiar with what your bees will be foraging on, pay close attention to when each plant is in bloom and also to when it seems as though nothing is in bloom or producing nectar or pollen. That period would be what beekeepers call "dearth." I know that I was not nearly as attuned to these cycles prior to keeping bees. This awareness of our hyper-local environment is one more gift from the bees.

CONVENIENCE: If your bee yard is horribly inconvenient to get to, you may not feel like providing the continual care that hives require. Site your apiary in a place you will enjoy working and that will not be hard to tote your beekeeping tools and equipment to and from. For most hobbyist beekeepers, this is somewhere right on their property or rooftop, although some beekeepers are able to establish small apiaries on neighboring properties or farms where the landowners want the benefit of pollinators.

It's important to also consider the convenience of your close neighbors. For obvious reasons, do not site a bee yard in a way that puts your neighbors' pool or their children's' play area in the direct flight path of your bees. Many inadvertent offenses can be smoothed over with a gift of fresh, delicious honey, but if your hives are a genuine nuisance to neighbors, more serious problems can ensue.

SPACE TO WORK THE HIVES: Especially if you are going to fence your bee yard, make sure that there is plenty of room for you to work the hives. Hives are inspected, treated, and worked from the back of the hive, never from the front where the entrances, and therefore the flight path of the bees, are. You will want to have plenty of room especially behind the hives for you, for anyone working the hives with you, and for your equipment. You will also want enough room in front of the hives to also get around them and plenty of room to add additional hives as your beekeeping venture grows.

PLATFORM HEIGHT: Your hives should be at least six inches off the ground on an almost level platform, but you can make them higher depending on your own comfort preferences. Remember that during inspections and during honey harvesting, you will be lifting boxes of various weights so if they are too low or too high you can run in to problems. I say the platform should be almost level because it's helpful to tilt the hives ever so slightly forward so that any moisture runs out "the front door" at the bottom of the hive, however, you do not want them tilted beyond that needed to accomplish drainage. This is because as the hives get higher during the season, as you add additional boxes and supers, you don't want the hives to be prone to tipping over. Our hive platform at the Parris House is made from cinder blocks set in a vertical orientation with two 4x4s laid across them to form a sturdy base. This platform holds four hives.

Pick Up Day and Installation

Our most recent package installation took place during a driving snow/sleet storm, in April, in Maine. I am going to admit that I was beside myself. I thought I was going to cry, which is super inconvenient when you're wearing a beekeeper's veil. Our bee packages had recently arrived from a bee rearing farm in the sunny and warm American South. These bees had no idea about snow/sleet storms…in April… in Maine. Frankly, I had no idea about installing bees under such harsh conditions either. We'd always had relatively nice days in past seasons.

Fortunately, our bee mentors are models of calm. They gave us a few pointers on minimizing the bees' exposure to the conditions during installation and away we went, ending up with our most successful season of beekeeping to date. I should note here that once bees arrive to your retail bee farm or shop, it is not desirable to delay installing them. Had the weather been too much worse we could have tried to perhaps keep them one more day in the packages, but it is best for their health and wellbeing to be installed into a waiting hive as soon as is practicable.

Hopefully now that you know that you can install bees successfully under relatively terrible conditions, you will feel a little more confident no matter what the weather when it is your turn.

To Install Your Package Bees, You Will Need:

- Bee packages (we recommend at least two)
- Prepared hives
- Perimeter shims to go between the upper box and inner cover if baggie feeding, an extra hive body (box) if jar feeding
- Spray bottle with sugar water
- Hive tool
- 1:1 sugar syrup ready in jars or baggies
- Smoker (use sparingly, if at all)
- Your bee suit/jacket and veil
- Your bee gloves, if desired
- Small knife

Especially if this is your first installation, take three deep breaths and review exactly what you are going to do once you're in the bee yard. It always helps to be calm, collected, and have a plan not only for bee installation but every time you work with your bees from this point forward.

Light your smoker and make sure it's not going to go out during the installation. This means it must be well lit. Give it a few puffs occasionally to keep it going and to make sure it's still lit. You don't need much, if any smoke, during the installation of package bees. They have little to defend. Like swarms, they are not defending an established hive and are generally docile. I found that having the smoker lit was more to give myself a feeling of security – "I can smoke them if they seem agitated! Or if I seem agitated!" – than any-thing else. I'm not sure we've used it at all during our own installations.

A note on smoker fuel: We use linen scraps from my rug hooking as smoker fuel, however, other common fuels are burlap, pellets made specifically for smokers, or just plain organic material like leaves, pine needles, small sticks, et al. It is important that the smoke coming out is not hot, how-ever. The smoke should feel relatively cool on your hand. If it is hot it can injure the bees. Additionally, do not use any-thing in the smoker that could possibly be toxic to the bees when burned.

Bring your packages to the bee yard. You are going to install them one at a time.

Open the first empty hive. Remove the outer cover, the inner cover, and one to three frames, your preference depending on how much room you think you'll need for installing the queen cage.

If it is warmish outside, perhaps 55 to 60 degrees Fahrenheit or higher, give your bees a little sugar spray through the wire mesh sides of your packages. This calms them down a bit and gives them something to do. Spritzing them in colder weather is not recommended because you don't want to chill your bees.

With your hive tool, pry the exterior wooden lid off of your first package. The bees will not come flying out! They can't because their feeder can is still lodged in the opening and the queen cage tab is wedged between it and the side of the opening.

I repeat...the queen cage has a tab that is sticking up and around the top of the feeder can. This is very important!

When you remove the feeder can, be sure to hold on to that tab and bring the queen cage out with it. Do not drop the queen in her queen cage into the interior of your package box. If you do, you are unlikely to have harmed her, however, you are likely to raise your new beekeeper anxiety level if you have to reach into the box of bees to bring her out again.

Once you have the feeder can and the queen cage out of the box, just set the wooden lid you pried off earlier over the package opening. This keeps most of the bees inside the package while you're installing your queen cage in the new hive. Place the feeder can on the ground near the entrance of the hive for now and hang on to that queen cage and hold it over your open hive.

You may have bees clustered around the queen on the queen cage. They are attending to her and this is a good thing. Just shake or brush the attending bees down into the open hive and then take a good, but quick look at your queen. Make sure she appears active, has all of her legs, and, if you ordered her marked, take a good look at that marking and what she looks like. This will serve you well if you are looking for her later in the season, which you often are.

IF your queen looks sick, lame, or worst of all, dead, contact your package provider immediately for instructions on replacement.

The queen cage has at least one, usually two, corks in it. One is at the lower end, opposite the tab end. Behind that cork you will see, through the mesh, a little white block of candy. With your small knife, remove the cork on that end only! The idea here is that the bees will eat through that candy in a time frame suitable for the queen to be accepted by the other bees. Once that opening is eaten through, the queen can walk out of the cage and start her work of laying eggs in any comb that is adequately drawn by then. Were you to remove the cork at the other end at this time, which is used to release a queen later that is not released naturally, you would risk the queen being killed because there had not been adequate time for the bees to accept her. So, remember, always look for the candy end when removing the cork on installation.

You are now going to attach the queen cage to an exposed frame, somewhere toward the middle of the upper hive box. There are several ways to do this, but the way we like best is to simply wrap the tab over the top of the frame and put a heavy push pin into it to hold it in place. Make sure there is at least one side of the cage mesh exposed, in other words, not pressed up against the frame, so that her attendants can continue to feed and tend the queen prior to her release into the hive.

Now it's time for the part I like best, literally pouring the rest of the bees into the hive. Do not be intimidated by this. As I said, they are generally very docile at this stage of things. Remove the cover you had placed loosely on the package box, center it over the open hive, flip it over, and gently pour, with a little bit of gentle shaking, the bees into the open hive. They will start releasing a pheromone letting the other bees know, "Hey, we got the queen right here!" and bees in the air will be alerted to also enter the hive. While you want to get as many bees into the hive as you can, don't worry if there are still some left in the package box. Just set that down in front of the hive and they will be attracted in over the course of the next hour or so.

Once most of the bees are in the box, you can replace

MAINE MAPLE SUNDAY

Maine Maple Sunday, or, as it's quickly becoming, Maine Maple Weekend, happens on the third weekend of March each year, usually just after the spring equinox. As such, it is an extremely early spring event and the weather can range from cold and snowy to muddy and balmy. Often it is a combination, with the morning below freezing and then warmer sunshine in the afternoon turning the farm lanes to a deep, boot-sucking mud..

There are about one hundred sugar houses open across the state of Maine on Maine Maple Sunday and many families, ours included, map out a route and visit several in a day or over the entire weekend. Each location has unique offerings and attractions, including, but not limited to, education and demonstrations, pancake breakfasts, maple syrup on ice cream, maple syrup snow cones, farm animals for petting, horse and carriage rides, farm tours, live music, and of course, the

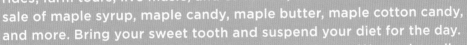

sale of maple syrup, maple candy, maple butter, maple cotton candy, and more. Bring your sweet tooth and suspend your diet for the day.

We don't have a sugarbush at the Parris House. We are in a village setting and simply do not have the land required for this. We do have family across town who have ten acres with sugar maples on them and have considered tapping their trees to boil down our own maple syrup. Still, you do not need a farm or an extremely large piece of land to do maple sugaring. Some of the stops along the Maine Maple Sunday tour are just residences with modest stands of sugar maples and sugar shacks no larger than a garden shed housing their evaporating equipment. Maple sugaring is a relatively accessible activity and I'd encourage you to try, even if all you have is a few sugar maples and a well-ventilated kitchen.

the frames you took out at the beginning of the installation, however, just place them gently down in to the hive and let them lower all the way as the bees vacate the areas underneath them. Jamming them back into the hive and pushing them down right away can kill any bees underneath, and we don't want that, especially with such a young colony. Adjust the frames to the proper width apart, making sure there is plenty of room for the attendants to care for the queen. Some beekeepers leave a frame out during the queen cage/acceptance period. We do not, but we do make sure there is room for her to be cared for through the mesh sides of the queen cage.

Next, you must put feed on the hive. Especially if these bees are going into brand new hives with empty frames, they have nothing for sustenance, therefore you must feed them. Usually this early in the season there is not enough forage and they are a young colony in need of energy just to draw the wax cells over all the brand-new frames. The recipe for spring feed is just 1 part table sugar to 1 part water, or 1:1 sugar syrup. It is not necessary to make this very complicated. Just fill half of a gallon jug with sugar and half with warm to hot water and shake until completely dissolved. Some beekeepers like to make the syrup stovetop to be absolutely sure that all the sugar dissolves. We do not. We simply mix as described, cool it to room temperature, and feed.

Note: As I mentioned, one year we had to install our bees in a sleet storm, as is not unheard of in New England. In that case we served the feed lukewarm because we knew it would raise the temperature inside the hive and help the bees, with a relatively small population and therefore limited ability to cluster for warmth, survive the cold snap.

There are two types of feeders we like at the Parris House apiary, and I say two types because I prefer one and my husband prefers the other. I like baggie feeders and my husband likes jar feeders inside the hive, over the inner cover. I'll provide a description of each and the pros and cons, but first I want to say that we do not prefer front feeders attached to exterior of the hives. Here's why.

Where we live, we are continually battling predators. During our learning curve, which is pretty much never-ending with beekeeping, we have had other syrup guzzling insects, voles, mice, and raccoons who wanted whatever was in our hives. To our knowledge, we have not yet had to contend with bears, but we take precautions, nonetheless. We feel that putting the sugar syrup right out in the open at the front of the hives is just an invitation to unwanted visitors in the apiary. Exterior feeders are a great convenience for the beekeeper and also let you observe, without opening the hives, when to replace the feed, but for us that convenience is simply not worth the risk. Since we do have to open the hives with our method to check and/or change feed containers, we just make sure that we are as unobtrusive and quick as possible, which is the mode you want to be in whenever you're in a hive for any reason anyway.

OK, so let's talk about what we do like.

Baggie Feeders

I like baggie feeders. These require one extra part for the hive, a rectangular shim about an inch high that goes between the top of the hive body and the inner cover. You fill a water-tight gallon size zipper lock baggie with sugar syrup, lay it horizontally across the top frames, and then ever so carefully make a two to three inch slit in the top with a sharp knife or box cutter. Dip your finger in to the opening and just get a little of the syrup out on to the baggie to attract the bees to it. Care must be taken not to fill the baggies so full that upon slitting they pour syrup through and out the bottom of the hive, but that they are rather at a level where the syrup lies just underneath the slit and the bees take it tiny sip by sip until the bag is empty. Replace the inner cover, on top of the shim, over the baggie, then put on the outer cover.

When the baggies are empty, just replace them with new ones, or if you are an utterly frugal Yankee like one of my mentors, you can use a funnel to refill them in place. In true Mainer style, he puts the syrup in an old gallon whiskey bottle and then funnels it in to the existing baggies.

PROS:

- Easy to use.
- No extra hive body or box is needed to contain them, just a shim to make room.
- Robbing by other bees/insects is minimized because the feed is inside the hive.
- Very inexpensive, especially if you are reusing the bags.

CONS:

- It is possible to overfill, especially when you are inexperienced, and have syrup leak through and out the front entrance of the hive, possibly attracting robbers. If this occurs, rinse down the spill area in the front of the apiary to discourage robbers.
- If you don't reuse the bags, you must make sure you always have the right ones on hand.
- You'll have bees all over the top frames when you are trying to lay down a new baggie, and some can be crushed in the process. A solution to this is to lay the baggie down slowly, starting with one end and allowing the bees to move out of the way. You might also just gently brush or smoke as many bees as possible out of the way before placing the baggie.
- Plastic baggies are not very environmentally friendly.

- You must remove the inner cover and slightly disturb the bees to place and replace the feed.

Interior Jar Feeders

This is my husband Bill's preferred feeding method. These also require an extra part for the hive, another entire hive body/box to sit between the inner cover and the outer cover.

Fill a quart jar with sugar syrup. Take a jar lid and punch it full of tiny holes, perhaps a dozen or so, so that when you put the lid on and turn the jar upside down, the vacuum created stops the syrup from pouring out but allows the bees to sip the syrup that beads around the holes.

Place the inverted syrup jars over the center hole of the inner cover, add a hive body/box to contain it, and then top with the outer cover.

PROS:
- Easy to use.
- Quart sized canning jars are washable and reusable.
- Glass jars are environmentally friendly.
- No need to remove inner cover or disturb bees when placing or replacing feed.
- Jars can be used for other homestead purposes between bee feeding seasons.
- Robbing is minimized because the feed is contained inside the hive.

CONS:
- An extra hive body/box is needed on each hive to contain the jars.
- Glass jars are breakable and occasionally can be dropped in the apiary, causing not only the mess, but the danger of broken glass.
- The considerable extra space created between the

inner and outer cover sometimes leads the bees to start wasting their energy and resources building brace comb, but this can be minimized by checking and scraping any errant comb frequently.

So, choose whatever method of feeding you prefer and make sure you keep your bees in plenty of feed until the nectar flow starts in earnest in your area and you see the corresponding increase in the amount of pollen they are bringing in to the hives. We usually stop feeding when the dandelions pop and we can see that the bees have plenty of forage in all of the emerging plants. Consult your mentors on this because the timing of the first nectar flow can vary widely depending on area and the particular conditions in any given year.

Removing the Queen Cage

Between three and seven days after installation, you need to check to see if the queen has been released from the queen cage. Three to four days is about the time we usually check. It is very important that the queen be accepted by the worker bees before she is released into the hive so that she is not killed by the rest of the colony. However, there are good reasons to release a queen at three to four days post-installation if the bees have not already chewed through the candy and released her. One is that it's best to have the queen start laying as soon as possible in a new colony and she may take a couple of days after release to begin. This is important because you don't necessarily know the age of the worker bees that came with her. The sooner she begins laying and the colony starts raising new bees, the less chance that many of the original package bees will die off before the new bees emerge to take over the workload.

So, what are some good indicators that the queen has or has not been accepted? If the queen is still in the queen cage, the candy is barely touched, the bees are "balling" around her, and possibly even biting at the wire, I would not release her. This is not typical acceptance behavior. Give it a few more days. However, if it appears that the bees are feeding the Queen, chewing away at the candy in the end of the cage, and attending to her calmly, go ahead and release her.

Once the queen is released, either naturally or with your help, remove the queen cage from the hive, make sure the spaces between the frames is even, and close the hive up.

Congratulations! Your bees are installed, and you know how to feed them as needed. From here, regular inspections will be key to make sure that they are thriving, but once your queen is released leave them alone for at least a week, better two, before going into the hives again. Their entire journey has been very stressful and it's a good idea to let them settle in and start building their new home. Again, it is best to have a mentor to help you through the first year, but what you will be looking for during your first inspections going forward are:

- Drawn comb if your bees were installed on fresh, undrawn frames.
- Eggs, larvae, and capped brood. In other words, brood at different stages of development.
- Brood pattern. Is the queen laying in a relatively uniform and even way without skipping a lot of cells or worse, not laying at all? If you believe your queen is not laying, contact the source of your package or your mentor immediately.

Check the resources section of this book for some excellent books, websites, and beekeeping supply shops that can help you as your season progresses and, most importantly, get out there with experienced beekeepers and learn as much as you can.

McLaughlin Foundation Lilac Festival

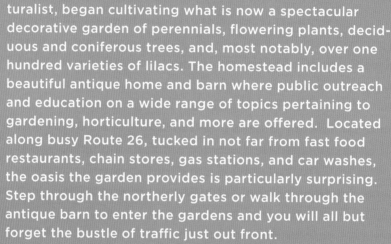

The McLaughlin Garden in South Paris, Maine, is one of the true gems of the region with a history that is a testament to the character of Maine and Mainers. Starting in 1938, Bernard McLaughlin, who was not a professionally trained horticulturalist, began cultivating what is now a spectacular decorative garden of perennials, flowering plants, deciduous and coniferous trees, and, most notably, over one hundred varieties of lilacs. The homestead includes a beautiful antique home and barn where public outreach and education on a wide range of topics pertaining to gardening, horticulture, and more are offered. Located along busy Route 26, tucked in not far from fast food restaurants, chain stores, gas stations, and car washes, the oasis the garden provides is particularly surprising. Step through the northerly gates or walk through the antique barn to enter the gardens and you will all but forget the bustle of traffic just out front.

Each year on Memorial Day weekend, the McLaughlin Garden hosts their Lilac Festival. Maine weather being unpredictable as it is, some years the lilacs are in full bloom and other years, not at all. We have found that our lilacs at the Parris House, which is only about three miles north and a few hundred feet higher than the McLaughlin property, bloom anywhere between around May 15th (at the earliest) and the first week or so of June and this varies unpredictably year to year. But not to worry. If you attend Lilac Festival in a year when the bloom is delayed, there is still plenty to enjoy. The earliest blooming plants are still fragrant and colorful, there is always a wonderful plant sale for augmenting your own gardens, and the garden's volunteers and full-time horticulturalist are on hand to give presentations and answer questions. There is a lovely gift shop filled with beautiful and unusual things, many made by local artisans.

The garden is open May through October and, while admission is free, it's great to make a donation in appreciation of this unique Maine sanctuary.

Preparing for and Establishing
Your Chicken Flock

Ordering Your Chicks

Before getting chicks, be sure that there are no local laws, ordinances, or homeowners' association restrictions on your having backyard chickens. I'm sorry to start out with this very important caveat, but in many more densely populated areas, this can be an issue.

Early in the new year you will start seeing your local farm stores and online hatcheries advertising the sale of baby chicks. This is an exciting time for us at the Parris House in the years we decide to augment our existing flock and will be an extremely exciting time for you if you are establishing your very first flock!

Our first flock of chickens was made up of six Golden Comets that were already well on their way to adulthood. At the time I was a full-time real estate broker and one of my officemates, Julie, had a daughter raising chicks for a 4H project. Julie asked if I'd like to purchase some of the young hens to support her daughter's project and to establish laying hens at the Parris House. Part of me thought, "Heck, yes!" and part of me thought, "I have no idea how to take care of chickens." Fortunately, my friend and her daughter were excellent tutors and we've had hens, and fresh eggs, for ourselves and for sale, at the Parris House ever since.

That was an excellent introduction to chickens for us. Having the chicks already raised to a size where they could be relatively independent in the coop before we got them allowed us to focus that first season primarily on preparing our coop. If you would like to take the process a little slower like we did, finding someone willing to sell well raised older chicks/young hens may be ideal.

However, there are advantages to ordering baby chicks and raising them yourself. For one, you will be able to watch the entire growth process from one- or two-day old hatchlings through adulthood. I joke that watching baby chicks grow reminds me of those novelty toys my sons had when they were little. These toys were tiny and when put in water would grow exponentially in a very short time in to either a larger toy or a small towel. Baby chicks need to be checked often when they first come home, and you will absolutely notice their growth in just an eight to twelve-hour period when they are very young. It's truly astonishing.

A second reason to raise baby chicks yourself is that you are socializing them to you and your family from literally their first days of life. It is much easier to have friendly, trusting hens than it is to have birds that are not accustomed to enough human contact and end up being skittish, defensive, or prone to pecking you. Well raised chicks from other chicken keepers will not be poorly socialized, but it is rewarding to do it yourself and develop a bond with them.

It's also fun to decide on breeds. In our flock we have a variety of cold climate hardy breeds that are not only a beautiful mix of predominant feather colors, but that also lay a variety of eggs, brown, dark brown, green, and blue green. By raising the chicks yourself you will be able to watch the feather development of each of the breeds you choose, which can be quite surprising. Your hatchery or farm store will have information on each breed, its disposition, adult size and weight, laying characteristics, egg color, cold hardiness, whether it also makes a good meat bird, and more.

You may or may not decide to name your chicks. We do not. We generally keep a flock of between twenty and thirty hens and naming them all would be challenging, to say the least. While we do not consider our hens strictly utilitarian livestock, they are also not exactly household pets. Where you fall on that continuum between livestock and household pets is entirely up to you, although I think the smaller the flock the easier it is to appreciate the individual personality traits that hens develop. Some hens have such strong personality traits that even in a flock of thirty or more, they may stand out. Our stand-out hens occasionally get a name, usually something a bit irreverent.

When deciding how many chicks to order, consider how much space you are willing to devote to a coop, how many birds you are willing to take care of, and how many eggs you want to have coming in daily when they are all laying at peak. Generally speaking, you will get one egg a day from each hen. Even with a small flock this adds up to quite a few eggs over the course of a week. There is always the option of selling your excess eggs but do check your state and local laws regarding selling backyard eggs prior to offering them for sale. Additionally, sometimes local food cooperatives will sell the eggs of individual, backyard chicken keepers.

Preparing Your Brooding Space and Bringing Your Chicks Home

Preparing the brooding space for your chicks need not be complicated, but you will want to make sure that the basic necessities for chicks are provided for. These are:

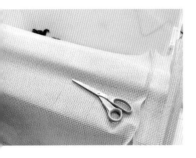

- Warmth
- Cleanliness/dryness
- Water
- Food
- Appropriate sizing of the space

Therefore, you will need:
- Heat lamp
- Clean bedding, larger pine shavings — NOT cedar
- Rubber shelf liner
- Paper towels or newsprint
- Waterers, preferably two with only one in the brooder at a time
- Feeder, may also have two, as above
- Chick feed, specifically formulated for chicks
- Plastic tub sized right for the number of chicks you are bringing home
- Wire mesh cover for the top of the brooder tub

We brood chicks in a clear plastic tote large enough to accommodate the shockingly rapid growth they experience in their first weeks. We top it with a metal mesh cover made from a simple wood frame with wire hardware cloth stapled to it, and place a heat lamp above it, close enough to keep them warm but not so close as to make the brood space hot. A good temperature range for chicks that have just come home is between 90 and 95 degrees, but you will also know if your chicks are too cold if they are spending most of their time huddling together for warmth. If they are too hot, they'll huddle as far away from the heat source as possible. If they are just right, they should be active, cheeping, hopping around the brooder, and eating and drinking. You can start moving the heat lamp a bit further away each week to reduce the temperature just a little bit, observing the chicks' behavior as you go to make sure they are comfortable.

We layer the bottom of the chick brooder this way: an old, soft, absorbent towel you don't care about on the very bottom, then some paper towels or the white paper I use for shipping (it's basically newsprint), then on top of that, rubber shelf liner which you can buy in rolls and clean each time you clean the brooder. The first week or so, omit the pine shavings as the last layer because tiny chicks can be confused about what is food and what is not, and you do not want them ingesting the shavings.

Even though it is easier to clean up, do not use just paper. This is a time when the chicks' feet are developing and growing stronger and they need to have something they can get a good grip on, not slide around on. If they do not have a good footing in the brooder at this age, they can develop a problem called spraddle leg, which will cause dislocation/deformity, making walking difficult to impossible, and can affect them for life if not treated. Treating spraddle leg is possible, however, it is much easier to try to avoid this particular cause of it. Adding the layer of grippy rubber shelf liner over the paper still allows the chick poop to drop through the holes and be absorbed underneath while giving the babies the firm footing they need.

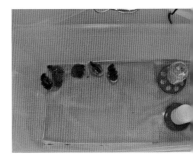

After a week or two, you can add pine shavings, however, do not use shavings fine enough for the chicks to ingest, because this can cause serious digestive problems. Do not use cedar shavings either because the oils in cedar are detrimental and possibly even toxic to baby chicks. There is no way around the fact that baby chicks, just like adult chickens, poop a lot, so once you add the shavings, you'll have one more layer of absorbency. You will need to change their litter frequently. We do it daily or, at the very least, every other day while the chicks are in the brooder.

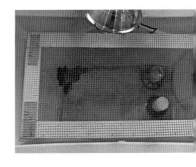

Fresh, clean water is very important to your chicks' health. It's nice to have two waterers on hand because ideally, you're going to change them often, sometimes twice a day. Having two allows you to remove the soiled one and immediately place the clean one. You can then wash the first one and have it ready for the next water change. When you first bring your chicks home, gently dip their beaks in the waterer, one at a time, so that they immediately get the idea for where to drink.

On the first day you bring your chicks home, just allow them water for the first hour or so. Allow them to hydrate, because they've likely been on a long journey and haven't had much access to normal, healthy amounts of water. Then introduce their feed.

Feeders also have to be kept clean, so if you want to have two of those on hand for the same purpose that's fine. Your chicks will be eating a specially formulated chick feed. Many feed companies recommend that you do not introduce treats to your chicks until they are several months old. If you do, and the treats are soft plant material and the like, then a grit would be needed to help them digest those but check with your feed store before introducing anything but chick feed. We do not offer our chicks treats until they are large enough to enjoy them with the larger, adult flock.

As your chicks grow, you will have to keep a vigilant eye on their food and water status. If it's out, refill it. If it's dirty, clean it. These are baby animals, after all, and they require a lot of care and attention at the beginning of their lives. If you are going to be going away even overnight, train someone to care for them while you are gone so that they cannot run out of clean water or food or be exposed to a very soiled environment.

In the first week of your chick's life at home, be on the lookout for a condition called "pasty butt." It's just what it sounds like. The chicks can get impacted feces that block their vents, prevent them from pooping, and allow toxins to build rapidly in their bodies. This is very quickly fatal if untreated. In the many years we have kept chickens, we have never encountered this firsthand, however, we're just lucky because this is not uncommon.

Should you unfortunately have a chick develop pasty butt, wet a q-tip and gently clear away the hardened feces from the vent. Do not be tempted to bathe the chick because they cannot regulate body temperature, especially when wet. Once you have the vent completely cleared, dab a bit of olive oil on the vent area to help keep it clean and clear. Monitor the chick carefully for recurrence and, of course, monitor the others in case they develop it also.

One way to try to prevent pasty butt is to keep the chicks' environment clean, stress free, and at a comfortable temperature. Do not feed them anything that could cause diarrhea or indigestion, another reason not to offer what we may perceive as treats until the babies are considerably older.

As I said, your chicks are going to grow exponentially in the first weeks and months. It is very important to make sure that they have enough space in the brooder. Should it start to appear that they are cramped, you can get them a larger brooder box, by either connecting more than one plastic tub (you can cut a doorway between two or more), building or purchasing a larger box, or getting something like a large livestock feeding/watering tub in which to house them. Do not separate them, however. It is best to keep your chicks together as a flock as they grow.

Moving Your Older Chicks to the Coop

Once your chicks are fully feathered out and too large for the brooder, it's time to think about moving them to the outdoor coop. We don't do this prior to the chicks being six weeks of age, even though that often means we have to create more brooder space for them. We also make sure that the temperatures outside are at least in the 60s, even at night. Predation prevention is extremely important at this stage. Chickens are relatively defenseless from most predators when they are full

grown let alone when they are still young like this.

This is also a time to start thinking about changing their feed from starter mash to grower feed. They can be switched over to grower feed between eight and ten weeks of age and then to layer feed when you see the first eggs at approximately eighteen to twenty weeks of age. Most grower feeds are not pre-gritted so you should add grit to this feed, especially if you are also feeding your chicks treats.

Preparing Your Coop and Run Space

You might decide to make your chicken coop cute. We do not. We do not decorate the coop with curtains, adorable signs, wallpaper, or other trinkets. Having said that, I thoroughly enjoy seeing coops that are completely decked out and if this is something you'd love to do, do it! The caveat is just to be sure that anything you use for coop décor is nontoxic and safe for your hens and that it is easily cleaned. Chicken coops are naturally dusty and, well, contain quite a bit of poop, so you just want to keep your décor clean and fresh for everyone's wellbeing.

We are fortunate to have a large room at the back of our barn that has been a chicken coop for generations. It can be accessed from inside, from the house by going through the garage and then to the barn, which is very convenient in winter. It can also be accessed via a large exterior barn door and there is yet another opening at the back of it that allows the chickens to exit to their outdoor enclosed run.

Our outdoor run backs up to the bee yard which provides a little extra protein treat for the hens when the occasional bee dies within their reach or when we have scraped brace comb containing a few brood cells from inside the hives. We also feel that at the height of the summer, the considerable presence of flying bees so close to their run may deter some predators. It does not disturb the hens one bit, although we do make sure that the hens' water source is not where the bees will also be drawn to it as the birds try to drink.

Having a hen house built into an attached barn, or even having an attached barn, is not the most common scenario, however, so you may need a different solution. Whether you are fortunate enough to have a barn or outbuilding like ours already or need to build one, some considerations are the same.

First, consider the size of your flock or potential flock if you plan to have more than your initial number of chicks. The general rule of thumb for space per bird is two to four square feet inside the coop. The more space you give your hens, the less likely it is that they will suffer potential consequences of overcrowding, which can be uncleanliness, disease, and aggressiveness or pecking. So, for example, if you are starting with six chickens, as we did, you would need at least between twelve and twenty-four square feet. I think it's a good idea to err on the side of giving them more room if you can, especially if you think you may eventually want to increase the size of your flock.

Second, consider the size of your predator-proof outdoor run space for them. Factory farmed hens, of course, often do not have any outdoor space at all, or even enough indoor space to do much more than turn around, but we want our hens to have a happy, natural life. It's therefore important for them to have ample outdoor grazing, dust bathing, and exercise space that they can use year-round. This space should also be covered over the top to keep out hawks and owls which can easily carry off a chicken. We let our hens outdoors to their run even in the Maine winter, often throwing them vegetable scraps, meal worms, and other goodies to peck at in the snow. Their outdoor run area does not have to be huge.

Ideally, it would be large enough for grass and other plants to keep pace with their scratching, foraging, and pecking. However, if it becomes a bit denuded at the height of the summer season, consider laying down straw, giving them lots of vegetable scraps to eat and peck at, and plenty of treats.

Free ranging your hens outside of an enclosure is a risky business. We never free range our flock in spring. This is because this is the time of year we see foxes, coyotes, fisher cats, raccoons, and other predators very near our home. They are hungry after winter and they often have offspring to feed. Your chickens are the perfect meal for them. We once made the mistake of free ranging our hens in spring, directly outside of our kitchen dooryard, heard a commotion and ran outside just in time to watch one of our hens being dragged away by a red fox. Only a trail of feathers remained of her.

Having said that, at other times of year, free ranging under your and/or perhaps a trusted dog's watchful eye can be very enjoyable for both you and your hens. Just always be vigilant and be aware that herding them back into their enclosure or coop prior to sundown, when they naturally return to their roosts, can be a bit like herding cats. We often find that carrying a bowl of vegetable scraps outside can turn us in to the Pied Piper of chickens, but this is not always the case.

Third, your hens need something to roost on. They do not like to be on the ground level of the coop most of the time. They will need a long enough roost, either in one long expanse or several combined, to have plenty of room between each bird. Allow about a foot per bird.

Roosting is a very natural behavior for hens so when you are in your coop toward the end of the day, counting heads, always be sure to look up too. Our hens enjoy roosting just on top of the open door to the hen house, which has resulted in their dropping surprises on my husband's head when he's gone to close the door.

Fourth, your hens need nesting boxes. A common rule of thumb is to provide at least one nesting box per four laying hens. This is where you can expect them to lay their eggs and where you will do most of your egg collection every day. They will lay in other odd places from time to time. We have cleaned out our coop and found a little cache of eggs in a corner somewhere, but the majority of the hens are laying in the nest boxes. At the Parris House we have an average of about 24 hens and we have ten nesting boxes, so a generous hen to box ratio.

Fifth, and most importantly, your coop must be predator proof and as vermin proof as possible. Predators are clever and can get through much smaller openings than you'd imagine. Our coop area has chicken wire and then flashing and boards on the underside, for example, because we discovered that predators could still get in through a very small gap from the underside of the barn. Any potential opening should be evaluated and closed up.

A notable coop option that is becoming increasingly popular is the chicken tractor. This is not a little farm tractor driven by chickens, although I sincerely wish such a thing existed. This is a wheeled, portable and secure chicken enclosure, sometimes including coop space and sometimes not, that can be moved around your property so that your chickens can always be safely foraging on a fresh patch of yard. This is brilliant because it keeps the chickens in fresh plant and insect forage, it keeps their droppings from accumulating in a single place, and therefore it is possibly cleaner and healthier for them than a stationary run. We do not have a chicken tractor at the Parris House...yet.

IN SUMMARY:
- Provide at least 2-4 square feet per hen inside their coop

- Provide as much space as you can for their secure, outdoor enclosed run
- Provide at least 1 horizontal linear foot of roost space per bird
- Provide at least 1 nesting box per 4 hens
- You must be sure your coop and run are predator proof

Special Instructions for Integrating New Chickens Into an Existing Flock

Young chickens cannot just be added to a coop full of older hens without risking trouble. Chickens have a pecking order and may not be kind to newcomers, so care must be taken to introduce new chickens using a few easy steps.

Create a separated space where the new hens and old ones can see and smell one another, but not directly interact. In our barn coop, we put up a chicken wire walled off area for our young chickens to live in while everyone becomes aware of one another. You could also have a large wire crate that you could put the young hens in within the larger coop with the older hens. Let them acquaint themselves with one another in this way for at least two weeks.

Allow a little mixed outdoor time. This should be supervised, especially at first. Put the new chickens in with the old chickens in the outdoor run and see how they interact. Do not allow anyone to be bullied and separate the hens if there is any danger of this. If the bullying is significant, keep the hens in their separate coop spaces for a few days to a week longer and try again.

This next step can be viewed as controversial, but it has never, ever failed us at the Parris House. Once the young chickens and older hens are well introduced and have gotten to know one another via their separate coop areas, and there is little or no conflict during the mixed outdoor time, we do nighttime integration. We wait until our older hens are asleep, we slip the young'uns into the coop, and when everyone wakes up in the morning it seems as though no one is the wiser. Having said that, at least for the first week keep a close eye on your newly integrated flock to make sure the young birds are accepted and holding their own. In over a decade of chicken keeping, this method has always worked for us.

Once you have all the birds successfully in one space, it's important to make sure your young hens are still eating their grower food. Therefore, you must feed everyone, including your older hens, grower feed until all the young hens have started laying. This will not harm your older hens and eliminates the literally impossible task of keeping two sets of hens eating two types of food. Once everyone is laying you can resume laying feed in the coop.

Cleaning an Established Coop after Winter

Perhaps you've already had chickens for a while and you're wondering just how clean that coop needs to be. As I said before, we don't make our coop cute. Our coop is utilitarian but clean and comfortable and we don't think our birds notice the decor. I do, however, think that for the health of your flock and for your health in working with them and eating their eggs, it's important to keep the coop as clean as you possibly can. Here is what we do in the spring, and at intervals throughout the rest of the year as best we can (winter brings serious limitations) to make sure our hens are happy, healthy, and clean.

Pick a warm, sunny day for the big coop-clean and start early in the morning so that your coop will have time to dry after cleaning and before your hens' bedtime. You'll also be

drying accessories outside in the sun, plus letting fresh air into the coop.

Do not use household cleaners in the coop. This is completely unnecessary and has the potential to make your chickens ill. If you feel you must use something as a cleaner, try white or apple cider vinegar mixed in a bucket of hot water. It's harmless, freshens up the coop, and is much cheaper than commercial cleaning products.

Send your hens out to play in their enclosed run or, if you're confident you can protect them while you work, let them free range. DO NOT LEAVE HENS UNATTENDED FREE RANGING IN EARLY SPRING! I cannot emphasize this enough. Predators have young to feed and food is relatively scarce for them this time of year. They will take your chickens right in front of you. I have, unfortunately, witnessed this and it is a scene never forgotten. I personally err on the side of not free ranging them at all in early spring, whether I can be right there with them or not.

If your coop is cute and you have curtains, signage, or other decorative items, get them all out and wash them.

Remove feeders and waterers and clean them thoroughly. White vinegar and hot water are a great combination for cutting through dirt on these. Let them dry in the sun.

Muck out old litter as completely as you can. NOTE: There is a "deep litter" method that can be especially useful in winter in which new litter is introduced often on top of old litter. To its credit, this is believed to introduce beneficial microbes that compost the litter in the coop as long as both you and the hens are keeping it "turned," you by occasional light raking and your hens by scratching at it. In the warmer months, however, we prefer to change their litter as nearly completely as possible, and this is springtime, so get on the muck boots, grab a shovel and pitchfork, and get all that old litter out of there.

You may find old eggs laid in odd places as you're muck-ing. Don't eat or sell these. There is no way to know how old they are or if they're safe. We put ours in the compost bin.

Remove all litter and nesting materials from your nesting boxes. Our old classic steel nesting boxes have bottom panels that pop out, making this a very easy process.

Get the shop vac out if you have one. Otherwise, go old school and use a broom. Sweep the walls, ceiling, corners, everywhere you can to remove excess dust and cobwebs that may have accumulated over the seasons.

Get the coop wet. This is another reason to do this job on a warm, sunny, dry day. We have a good-sized coop and we hose out the interior, with a fair amount of water pressure, to really remove dust, caked on dirt, and get a truly fresh start to the season. While the coop is wet, we scrape any areas that look like the dirt and waste are not yet off. This includes roosting areas, densely soiled areas of the floor, or anywhere else we might find stubborn dirt. We use a hoe to do this and fortunately, there is not generally much of it to do.

Use a scrub brush, in your hand and/or on a pole, to scrub down the walls, ceilings, and floor.

You may hose the interior down one more time to rinse off anything loosened in this process. Then with all coop windows and doors wide open allow it to dry completely. Do not put your fresh litter or your hens back in the coop until it is completely dry.

When everything is dry, put your fresh litter of choice down on the coop floor and in the nest boxes. If you are concerned about mites, you may also mix in some diatomaceous earth with the floor litter and sprinkle a little in the nest boxes too.

If your coop has any electrical power to it, usually for lighting, now is a very good time to do a safety check on it. Inspect wiring, outlets, and bulb sockets to make sure every-thing is in good, non-worn condition and cannot be pecked

or otherwise damaged by your flock. Coop fires are utterly tragic in themselves and if your coop is in an attached barn, like ours is, fire can threaten the entire complex, including your home, and threaten your life. It's worth it to do a safety check several times a year.

Reinstall your feeder, waterer if you use it inside the coop, and décor, if you have it, and let your hens in to inspect and approve your hard work. This is also a great opportunity to give them a few treats and enjoy some social time with them in their new sparkling clean environment.

NOTE: There are three common chicken keeping practices we do not engage in at the Parris House: keeping a rooster, incubating fertile eggs ourselves, and turning our hens in to meat birds. For expert advice on any of these practices I would refer you to the many other chicken keeping and homesteading resources available.

Here's why we don't do those things.

KEEPING A ROOSTER: As noted, we live in a small village setting with relatively close neighbors. Roosters can be noisy and a little aggressive. While these characteristics often make them excellent flock guardians, they can also make them very bad neighbors. Crowing at dawn, and any other old time they feel like it, possibly chasing and/or pecking small neighborhood children, or even trying to prevent us from harvesting his ladies' eggs might well be considered a bit too anti-social for our environment. Because we keep our hens safe from predators in a secured environment, we'll skip having a rooster, his noise, and the extra feed he'd be consuming without producing eggs, eggs we'd rather not have fertilized.

INCUBATING FERTILE EGGS OURSELVES: Without a rooster, sourcing fertile eggs is slightly more complicated, although we know we could purchase some from other keepers with roosters or from a hatchery. We also like knowing that it's overwhelmingly likely that the chicks we purchase already hatched and professionally sorted are female. Finally, as a very small homestead engaging in a wide variety of activities, hatching our own chicks is not at the top of the priority list for us and we'd prefer to let a reputable hatchery do that job. Homesteading on any scale requires making decisions about what you want to do yourself and what you want to leave to others. In our case, hatching chicks is the latter.

RAISING MEAT BIRDS OR "RETIRING" HENS TO THE SOUP POT: The simple and honest answer is, we just can't. We cannot. We know how to humanely slaughter chickens, and there are plenty of good farmers in our area who would do the processing for us, but we choose to let them live. We fully support our friends and neighbors who raise meat birds and we do not have any moral objection whatsoever to the practice, especially when we know how humanely they are raised compared to factory farmed birds. I am, however, a vegetarian, and my husband, an omnivore, is simply unable to consider eating one of "the girls." (For those wondering, yes, he eats chickens he "hasn't met.") Therefore, we always have old hens in the flock, not technically earning their keep but living out their lives with our appreciation for the thousands of eggs they provided us throughout their lifetimes. Do I recommend this to others? Not necessarily. This is a very personal choice and again partially depends upon where you fall on that continuum between keeping chickens-as-pets and chickens-as-livestock.

Spring Projects

Vintage Look Fiddlehead Fern Hooked Table Mat and Coasters

This is the first of several hooked projects you will find in this book. (You can find a link to my website, where patterns and instructional videos may be found, in the resources section.)Rug hooking is my number one fiber art passion and the one that is the focus of my making and teaching life. It has a rich heritage as a North American art, having originated in New England and the Canadian Maritimes. Rug hooking was a craft of necessity in its earliest days in the nineteenth century when men and women fashioned hooked floor rugs from burlap sack foundation and worn out clothing cut into strips. From these very utilitarian beginnings, North American rug hooking has become a fine art/craft practiced all over the world, although its epicenter remains New England and the Maritimes. The project that follows is a simple introduction to rug hooking from which you will be able move on to more complex projects if you wish.

It's important to note rug hooking is always best learned with a teacher present, although self-taught hookers are not unusual. Because at Parris House Wool Works we ship rug hooking patterns, kits, and supplies all over the United States, I often find myself finding teachers in other areas for my customers. Google is a simple resource for this, although it is also good to contact ATHA, the Association of Traditional Hooking Artists, which has chapters all over the United States and can also help find a teacher near you. Should you have any questions about rug hooking or need help, I wholeheartedly invite you to contact me personally and I can help answer your questions or direct you to some-one nearby.

Fiddlehead ferns are a fun and easy design element that's perfect for spring and perfect for beginner rug hookers. Because the table mat and coasters are not that large and because the finishing technique is a simple pressing with a bonding material, vs a hand sewn method, the project is accessible and relatively quick to complete.

You Will Need

- rug hooking frame or thick edged quilting hoop
- basic rug hook
- paper pattern of the design
- black Sharpie or fabric marking pen
- linen, 16" x 30", with edges serged, zig zagged, or painters taped
- 1.5 fat quarters purple (or color of your choice) hooking wool (washed and fluffed)
- ½ fat quarter spring green hooking wool (washed and fluffed)
- purple or color of your choice mat and coaster backing wool, about a quarter yard
- Heat N Bond or some other kind of iron on bonding material
- clothes iron
- two colorfast hand towels

NOTE: Your wool must be washed and dried prior to cutting for hooking. Wash on gentle cycle in warm water then tumble dry on low. Do not overdry to the point where the wool felts. You want it to just be clean and slightly fluffed.

Making Your Pattern and Preparing Your Wool

Start with your linen piece. With your measuring tool (quilting square, ruler, or yardstick) measure a point 4 inches in from each side at the corner of your linen and make a dot with your Sharpie or fabric marking pen. For the table mat, measure 8 inches down the longer side and make another dot. Connect these dots NOT by putting a straight edge between them and tracing, but rather by running the tip of your marker directly down a single grain in the linen to form a perfectly straight and "on the grain" line. From the end point of that line, to form the next side of the square, make another dot 8 inches and again, create the next line by running your marker directly down a single grain of the linen. Continue in this way all the way around, four lines, until you have your 8" x 8" square. Next, draw your 4" x 4" coasters, four of them, two to a row, below your 8" x 8" square leaving at least 2 to 3 inches between them. You should also have 3 to 4 inches all around your drawn squares out to the edge of the linen, forming a generous allowance for putting it on your hoop or frame.

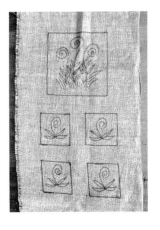

To keep the far outer edges of the linen from raveling while you are working on the rug, you must somehow secure them. You can do this either by using a serger/overlock machine on the edges, using a zigzag stitch on a conventional sewing machine (going around twice), or by simply putting some masking/painter's tape around the edges.

Trace the patterns onto the linen, doing the 8" x 8" table mat first followed by each of the 4" x 4" coasters. Place the appropriate paper pattern directly under the linen. Place the linen on top and align your square with the square edges on your linen pattern. If desired, pin the linen pattern in place to the paper pattern below, aligning the corners and edges to hold it in place correctly. Now, looking through the linen, trace the pattern from the paper onto the surface of the linen. For simple patterns, this is fairly easy to do. For more complex patterns, using a light box or table beneath, or using a transfer material like red dot can be more convenient. A light or white table surface helps in any case. Once you are finished tracing the mat and all four coasters, remove the paper pattern and your linen pattern is complete.

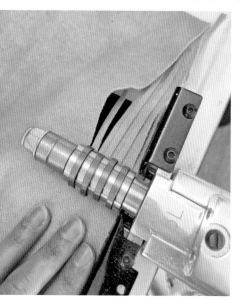

Cut your wool into strips, only enough for the project at hand because you want to save your whole wool leftover for future projects that might require a different size strip. We are using a size 5 strip for this project, which equals 5/32nds of an inch, but you might also choose size 6, or 6/32nds inch or even mix the two sizes, doing the more detailed work in 5 and the background in 6. The cutting can be done either with a wool cutter made specifically for this purpose, or it can be done by hand with a rotary cutter or with scissors. A wool cutter is recommended for easy, even strips. Wool cutters also come with dies or blades that will cut a variety of sizes, depending on what size you'd like to work with.

Hooking Instructions

You will need a quilting hoop (you want your hoop to be thick, at least an inch or an inch and a quarter high) or a rug hooking frame for best results. While some hookers have hooked without either of these, it makes the process much more challenging. Put your linen pattern on your hoop or frame. It is very important that you stretch the linen tightly so that you have a firm, tight work surface. Whether you are using a hoop or a frame, be sure to pull the linen as tightly as you can across the surface and secure it. Make sure you pull a little bit to the interior of the edges, and not directly on your serging, zig zagging, or tape as those can pull off relatively easily and your linen will ravel!

As a matter of planning how you will hook these pieces, it is best to "anchor" your edges first by hooking completely around the squares. In this case, hook one purple row on the outermost edge, one green accent row, and then another background color row completely around the interior of each square. Then proceed to the fiddleheads using the green wool. Background is filled in last by "echoing" your elements, hooking around them and then moving out in concentric rows.

You may hold your hook in your dominant hand in the traditional grip, which is handle end nestled in or toward your palm with thumb and forefinger gripping the base on the handle that attaches to the actual hook, or you may hold it in a regular pencil grip, whichever you find more comfortable. Your non-dominant hand holds the wool strip, or "worm" underneath the linen. To start, pull the end of the wool strip up through the linen at your starting point, which will be somewhere along one of the pattern lines. Always hook to the inside of the line, rather than on it or outside of it, to maintain the size and shape of your pattern elements. An exception to this is when you are hooking a single line

element, like our fiddlehead stems and curls in this project, which are hooked directly on the line. This first pulled up end will be a "tail." You want all tails, the pieces at the beginnings and ends of strips, to be on top of the linen, not hanging out below. Now, in the next hole along your pattern line, pull a loop topside instead. Continue pulling loops along your pattern line until you have outlined that element that you are working. Once your element is outlined, work inward in rows concentric to the shape until you reach the center and have filled the entire element. An example would be your fiddlehead leaf. Outline around the interior of the defining line and then fill in, working toward the center.

IMPORTANT NOTES FOR THE HOOKING PROCESS: Put the hook into the linen holes angled slightly from the side, not from directly overhead. This helps to prevent catching the hook on the linen as you exit the hole after pulling the loop up. Make sure that the wool strip is completely within the hook and that the hook is not trying to split it in the middle as you pull up. When starting a new strip where you have left off from the one before, start it in the same hole you left off from, creating two tails standing up from the same hole. These are snipped off even with the loops and visually disappear into the rug. Do not hook every hole. Hook every hole only while you can pull the next loop without having to reach under the one you just pulled. Skipping holes is normal and necessary to avoid packing the loops too tightly. The height of the loop should be approximately equal to the width of the strip, although this is a guideline and not written in stone. However, do not make the loops so low that they are easy to pull out from the reverse side.

Steaming and Blocking Your Project

When the pattern is completely hooked, take it off the frame and steam it. Place a towel down on a heat proof surface (ironing board or something similar) then put the finished rug on top. Put your iron on the wool setting. Get a second small towel, wet it thoroughly, and wring it out. Put the damp towel on top of the rug and now apply gentle pressure with the hot iron, tamping it down until you have done the entire piece. Do not slide the iron back and forth as you would on clothing. Lower and lift it from place to place. Do this also on the reverse side. You may need to re-wet the towel during this process. Steam will rise from the surface; be careful not to let this burn you. When you have done the entire piece, front and back, it will still be hot and damp. This is the time to pull the rug into "square" if it's not already, or just from the surface tweak with your fingers or the tip of your hook any loops or lines that don't seem aligned to you.

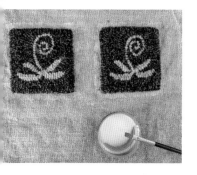

Finishing Instructions

Place your table mat and coasters (do not cut them apart yet) on a sheet of waxed paper. You are going to spread white glue all around the edges of your coasters and do not want the linen to stick to your surface. Waxed paper prevents this. To start spreading the glue you may put some of it in a disposable cup and brush it on with a small paint brush, a Q-tip, or your finger, or you may just run a bead of glue around the outline of the mat and coasters and then use your desired tool to spread it from there. Get the glue as close to the hooked edge as possible but try not to get any glue on the loops themselves. Spread the glue from the edge of the hooking to at least half an inch (up to an inch) out from that edge and onto the surrounding linen. Allow to dry (or use a low hair dryer to help dry it more quickly) and then flip the project over and do the same thing on the other side. The purpose of this step is to stop the linen from fraying on the finished piece.

When the glue is completely dry on both sides, you may cut your mat and coasters out, cutting along the outer edge of the glue. Leave a half inch to an inch of glued linen around the hooked area. Do not cut all the way to the hooked edge during this step!

Take out your plastic fabric bonding material (I used Heat n Bond Ultra Hold for this project) and trace the outlines of your mat and coasters on to it. Cut out the squares of bonding material and place them, plastic side down (paper side up) onto the backs of your coasters. Using an iron per the package instructions, press the bonding material onto the back of each coaster. You will now have a mat and four coasters with bonding material adhered to them, with the paper side of the bonding material still on.

Peel the paper off each mat and coaster back. You will now see that your mat or coaster has a plastic backing. The purpose of this is to prevent condensate from reaching the bottom side of the piece when it is in use.

Now it's time to put the wool bottoms onto the mat and coasters. Cut squares of your wool backing material slightly larger than your mat and coasters plus linen edge. Place the backing material onto the plastic back side of the mat and coasters. To protect the wool backing from the iron, place a damp cloth over it and then, again, use the iron to bond the wool backing to the plastic back of the mat and coasters. Once bonded, allow the pieces to cool and dry completely. Test the wool backing to make sure it is completely adhered to the mat and coasters. If not, repeat the ironing step until fully bonded.

Once cool, dry, and completely bonded, use a sharp pair of sewing shears to cut right along the very edge of the hooking on the mat and coasters. This may seem intimidating at first, but just be careful not to cut into any of the loops. Once complete, you will be able to see the layers of the pieces from their edges: hooking, linen, wool backing. You will not be able to see the thin plastic, however, that will serve as a waterproof center for your coasters. Your table mat and coasters are ready to use or give as a gift!

Apple Blossom Appliqué

This project is simple and easy. For me, it's also a reminder of the vintage décor I've seen in old Maine camps and farmhouses. Not long after we moved to Maine and my youngest son went to kindergarten, I decided to launch what would become a decade-long real estate career because of my love for homes of all kinds and my desire to help people find just the right one. During that time, I must have seen hundreds of houses, all around Maine. There was a particular type of interior décor referred to as "Goin' to Grandma's." This project is an homage to that décor style, but also a nod to today's modern cross-stitchers and punch needle artists who frame their work with embroidery hoops. Changing up the colors and base wool, or the style of framing hoop, can help make the result just right for your homestead.

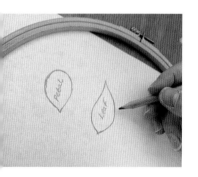

You Will Need

- A ten-inch embroidery hoop
- Background wool
- Flower wool, 2 shades
- Flower center beads and embroidery floss
- Leaf wool
- Perle cotton and/or embroidery floss in coordinating colors
- Embroidery needle
- Tapestry needle
- Embroidery and Sewing scissors/shears
- Templates for design elements
- Straight pins
- Embellishments (optional) – beads, embroidery floss, fine ribbon, et al

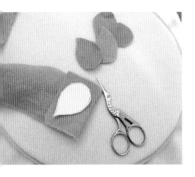

Directions

Have fun with this. Do not stress about placing the design elements exactly as I have placed mine. When I was a child one of my favorite things to play with were Colorforms sets. These were pliable plastic re-stickable design elements – objects, shapes, flowers, characters, etc. – that could be stuck any way you wished on to either a blank board or an established scene and then removed again for the next play session. This is kind of like that, only we're only "sticking" our elements down once. My point is, arrange the flowers any way you like, or follow the example. It's up to you.

Place your background wool tightly in to your hoop, spreading it evenly and creating a firm workspace for your applique.

Lay your design elements on the appropriate colored wools and cut around them with the small scissors to create the shapes in wool.

Pin the shapes on to your background wool in the configuration you like best. It is not necessary to pin these in place all at once; you can build the design as you go, pinning one or two, stitching them from there, and then adding as you go. It IS a good idea, however, to at least lay out the design initially, without pins, just to make sure it's going to center and fit the way you want it to.

Stitch your elements in place using the perle cotton. You can use a basic running stitch, a blanket stitch, or fancier stitches. In the example shown, I used running stitch, closed fly stitch, open chain stitch, and French knots. If you want to get fancy with your stitching, I recommend a comprehensive guide by stitching artist Sue Spargo in the resources section of this book, however, a perfectly attractive applique can be produced with the most basic of stitches.

Once all of your elements are stitched into place, you may choose to embellish them by stitching on beads, using iridescent embroidery floss, or whatever you can imagine giving it a little pop.

When finished, make sure the wool backing is still tight in the hoop. If not, pull it as tightly as possible and tighten down the hoop with a screwdriver so that the appliqued piece cannot move.

Trim the excess background wool to about an inch around the hoop, then thread a loose running stitch with floss or perl cotton through the entire cut edge, leaving long tails at the beginning and end points of the stitches. Pull the two ends tightly together to cinch the backing edge and tie with a double square knot. Your appliqued piece is now ready to hang or give as a sweet hostess or Mother's Day gift.

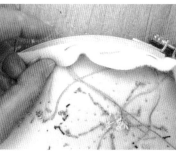

Gin & Tonic Bug Spray

Mid to late spring brings on what we not-so-lovingly call black fly season in Maine. Black flies, or what some people call "no-seeums," are tiny, swarming, biting insects that tend to be attracted to our exhale. Therefore, they are particularly bothersome when we are respiring quite a bit, for example when we are hiking, doing yard work, gardening, or otherwise exerting ourselves. However, don't be fooled in to thinking that they won't accost you if you're simply sitting outside, minding your own business. They will.

As a result, Mainers are forever trying different insect repellents to try to mitigate black fly season and also just keep mosquitoes at bay the rest of the year until the first hard freeze in the fall.

In recent years, people have become increasingly concerned about the chemicals used in commercial insect repellents, particularly DEET. I confess that if I am going for a true woodland hike any time from late April through September, I am likely to have a DEET product in my backpack. Lyme disease is a very real risk in New England and elsewhere and when I am doing serious outdoorsing, I do bring out the heavy artillery to ward off ticks, mosquitoes, blackflies, and whatever else is out there. I also realize that this is controversial, so fortunately, I have a lighter, more naturally derived, but still effective recipe for bug spray here that works well for me around the village homestead.

I call this formulation "Gin & Tonic Bug Spray." Unfortunately, it is not made of gin or tonic, which means that you cannot pull double duty with this and refresh yourself inside and out while gardening. If anyone would like to experiment with actual gin and tonic as insect repellent, please write me with the results.

The reason I named this insect repellent Gin & Tonic Bug Spray is because it contains essential oils with scents that remind me of my favorite cocktail. These oils are juniper, lemongrass, and lemon. (I realize the cocktail purists among you might insist on lime, but lemon and lemongrass essential oils are easier to find.)

You Will Need

- 12 ounces witch hazel
- 1 tablespoon citronella oil
- 1 teaspoon lemon essential oil
- 1 teaspoon lemongrass essential oil
- 1 teaspoon juniper essential oil
- 1 tablespoon plain vodka or rubbing alcohol
- glass spray bottle large enough to hold the contents or two or more bottles to split them
- waxed paper to protect your surface if desired

Citronella, lemon, and lemongrass oils are useful for repelling mosquitoes and blackflies. Juniper is included because it is repelling to ticks. This is a strong concentration of these oils. I call it "Maine strength." Therefore, as good as it smells, try not to inhale it directly and do not apply it directly to your skin. I'm going to say that a couple of more times before we're finished here.

Directions

1. Measure out 12 ounces of witch hazel and 1 tablespoon alcohol in a 2-cup measuring cup.
2. Measure out your oils into another measuring cup; it can be smaller. I recommend using glass whenever working with essential oils because some can etch plastic.

3. Combine the two measuring cups and mix thoroughly.

4. Use the narrow funnel to transfer all contents into the spray bottle or bottles, making sure it is well combined before stirring because the oils tend to separate a little from the witch hazel and alcohol. I used an 8-ounce bottle to keep in the house and a 4-ounce bottle to have in my purse or backpack.

5. Give the bottle a little shake each time before you apply the spray to thoroughly mix the oils with the witch hazel. Apply to articles of clothing, NOT directly on your skin.

NOTE: Insect repellent, "natural," DEET based, or any other type, should never be applied directly on the skin. I spray it lightly on to a bandana, baseball cap, my sweatshirt or hoodie, and down around my socks and pant cuffs. Even though natural formulations are often made with essential oils, it is important to note that these oils are not completely nonreactive on the skin. Depending on the person and the oil used, skin irritations, mild to severe, can result. Therefore, always apply to an article of clothing, not directly on your skin.

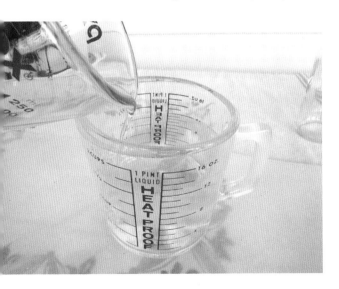

Spring Recipes

Spring recipes are a refreshing opener to the more bountiful seasons ahead. The earliest greens are making their appearances, Maine's maple sap has started to flow again, busying the sugar houses even as the snow is still melting, and the days are lengthening, increasing our flock's egg production. As in all seasons, using what's freshly available makes for the most delicious meals.

The recipes that follow make tasty use of some of the earliest vegetables we have in Maine: fiddlehead ferns, asparagus, rhubarb, and dandelion greens. Here at the Parris House we do not (yet) grow asparagus, but it is generally given to us by neighbors who do. We do have a single large rhubarb plant, a perennial, and because we fondly welcome dandelions on our property, for both their beauty and as excellent early forage for our bees, we have dandelion greens in copious quantity.

Sauteed Fiddleheads Over Dandelion Greens with Chevre

Fiddleheads are a Maine delicacy eagerly awaited every spring. They are not farmed, but rather foraged in the forested areas and along the edges of fields while they are still tightly curled, looking just as they are named, like fiddleheads. The most common edible species here in the Northeast is the Ostrich fern and should not be confused with other types of ferns that are not for eating. Edible fiddleheads have a papery exterior around them as they emerge. They are not the fuzzy type. It is important to either know your fiddleheads well or let someone who does do the foraging. Fortunately, here in Maine, fiddleheads can be purchased in the spring at farmers' markets, farm stands, and even the large supermarket chains, so if you are unsure just purchase some.

Prep time: **30 minutes**

Cook time: **15 minutes**

Serves: **4**

Next it is important to know how to pre-cook fiddleheads before even starting your recipe. Fiddleheads should be washed thoroughly as you would any other vegetable, but then it is important to cook out a potential toxin prior to consuming them. Failing to do this has been known to make some people sick. I prepare fiddleheads by boiling them for a few minutes, pouring out the water, putting fresh water in the pot and boiling again. I boil three times. Don't worry; they will not get overcooked, especially since the final part of the recipe is usually a quick flavorful sauté in olive oil along with anything else you'd like to add. If you do not have access to fiddleheads in your home area, you can use young asparagus as a substitute in the recipe here, without all that pre-boiling of course.

Also, let me just give you a quick word about dandelion greens: they're not for everyone. I like the bitterness of dandelion greens and I find that in this recipe the tangy lemon

juice and zest accompanied by the creamy, mild chevre seriously mitigates the bitterness. However, if they're just too strong for you, use arugula or any green of your choice. I pick our dandelion greens when they're on the smaller, tenderer side and then keep them fresh in a glass vessel with some cold water in it in the fridge for up to a day. I don't like to pick them too far in advance because they are best fresh. If you pick too many, you know what to do if you have chickens. Hens love dandelions and greens; it's a special treat for them.

Ingredients

1-pound fresh fiddleheads (or thin, tender asparagus if you cannot get fiddleheads)
2 tbsp olive oil
2 tsp fresh lemon juice
Pinch sea salt
4 cups fresh dandelion greens (or arugula or other greens, if you prefer)
4 ounces fresh chevre (goat cheese)
Lemon zest and dandelion blooms for garnish
Optional dressing: equal parts olive oil and lemon juice with a dash sea salt

Directions

1. Precook the fiddleheads by boiling for 2-3 minutes, drain, boil again, drain, if desired, boil and drain one more time.

2. Heat olive oil in an appropriately sized frying pan or cast-iron skillet. When hot, toss in the precooked fiddleheads and sauté until tender, around three minutes.

3. Toss in the pinch of sea salt and the fresh lemon juice.

4. Arrange on a bed of fresh dandelion greens, sprinkle with crumbled chevre, and garnish with a little (or a lot, if you prefer) lemon zest. If you have some, you could even add one or two dandelion flowers on the side for color and presentation.

5. If you want the recipe a little zestier, add the optional dressing to taste.

This recipe tastes like Spring to me. It's fresh, it's made with early, tender vegetables available only this time of year, and local goat cheese is also often made in spring when the mama goats have recently given birth and are being milked. Enjoy this lovely dish as a side or as a light main meal.

Parris House Spring Equinox Bread

Prep time: **2.5 hours depending on rise time**

Cook time: **30-40 minutes**

Serves: **6**

The traditional Italian Easter bread that I grew up with was a very sweet, almost Challah type bread with festive sprinkles on top and brightly colored Easter eggs adorning it. That bread, of which I have such fond memories, was the inspiration for this one. This bread can be used for an Easter celebration for sure, but if you do not celebrate Easter, it's also just a pretty harbinger of the arrival of Spring. It's also savory, instead of sweet, and I think this makes it a more versatile accompaniment for a wider range of meals.

I do not color the decorative eggs for this bread. We have a lovely assortment of dark brown, light brown, and blue/green eggs from the Parris House hens and I love the natural colors in the bread. However, I do find that plain white eggs look a little stark in this recipe, so if that is all you have access to, dye your eggs in whatever colors you love.

Bread dough ingredients

1 package dry yeast (or 1 Tbsp)
½ cup warm water
1 cup warm milk
1 Tbsp sugar
1 Tbsp olive oil
1 egg
1.5 tsp sea salt
½ cup whole wheat flour
3.5 cups bread flour (add more if
needed but be careful not to make
the dough tough)
½ cup fresh chopped dill

Decorating ingredients

6 raw eggs, colored or not (your preference)
3 Tbsp melted butter
2 Tbsp coarse sea salt

Directions

1. Combine the yeast and all the wet ingredients, the sea salt, and the sugar in a large mixing bowl and whisk them well.
2. Gradually mix in about half of the flours until you have a wet dough, add the chopped dill, then mix some more.
3. Add the rest of the flour and when you have a kneadable consistency turn the dough out on to a floured surface and knead it for several minutes until it starts to become more elastic and smooth.
4. Use a little cooking spray or oil to grease a large bowl and plop the dough down in to it.
5. Cover with a tea towel and place in a warm location to rise.

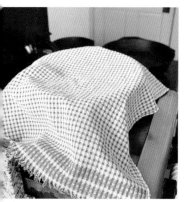

While the dough is rising, choose your decorative eggs. Let them sit out on the counter to come up to room temperature, or, if you are dyeing them, this would be a good time to do that.

PLEASE NOTE: the eggs must be raw. This is because they will cook in the oven when you bake the bread. If they are cooked beforehand, the shells will very likely split and the eggs inside will be chalky and dry from overcooking.

7. Once your dough has about doubled in size, punch it down and divide it in to three equal sized balls.

8. Roll the balls out into equal length and width ropes. Now it's just like braiding hair! Braid the dough and then form it into a circle, molding together the two ends. Don't worry if the connection point doesn't look pretty or braided; you're going to just put an egg in there anyway. Arrange the circular braid on to a well-greased baking sheet.

9. Be very careful with this next step because the eggs are raw and fragile and can break. Press the eggs into the connection point and then evenly spaced around the circle, tucking them in to the nooks of the braid.

10. Let the braided bread rise again, about forty-five minutes, in a warm place covered with a tea towel. It will almost double in size again and puff up around the eggs.

11. Once risen, it is time to prepare the bread for baking. Melt the butter and brush it on to the bread, taking care not to get any on the eggs because it will cause discolored spots while baking. Sprinkle a bit of coarse sea salt on the buttered area, again avoiding the eggs. If you do get sea salt on the eggs, they will speckle.

12. Heat your oven to 350 degrees Fahrenheit and bake on the top rack for 15 minutes, then move to the bottom

rack for another 15 minutes. I do this to avoid the bread browning too much on the top or bottom. Ovens differ, however, so keep a good eye on the bread to monitor browning. Time may vary oven to oven. The bread is finished when it is nicely browned top and bottom and a knife carefully put in to one of the braid points doesn't yield doughy results.

This bread is amazing served warm with a quality farm fresh butter or dipped in an herbed olive oil. Let the eggs cool down a bit before cracking them open for eating. If you are having spinach salad with your meal, the hard-baked eggs make a great topping for that.

Heritage Skills for Contemporary Living

Bill's Homemade Ice Cream with Strawberry-Rhubarb-Maple-Syrup Sauce

My husband Bill's family has used this French vanilla ice cream recipe for three generations. I love this recipe because it is exceptionally creamy and can be enjoyed plain or dressed up, as with the accompanying strawberry rhubarb sundae sauce sweetened with Maine maple syrup. The flavors of the sauce are pure Maine spring, with the tang of the rhubarb intentionally left as the predominant flavor tempered by the sweet maple syrup and strawberries. Strawberries are not a spring ingredient in Maine, so if you are also in a cooler climate just find the freshest, juiciest strawberries you can. This recipe is so delicious year-round, though, that it's just as appropriate for a July 4th or Canada Day celebration. Here in Maine we are still harvesting the smaller stalks of rhubarb in July and by then we also have fresh, delicious strawberries from local farms. At the Parris House on the 4th of July we serve this ice cream and sauce on top of blueberry pie, resulting in a red, white, and blue dessert.

The sundae sauce can also be used in other ways. It's a great waffle and pancake topping, good stirred in to plain or vanilla yogurt, and could also be incorporated into smoothies.

You will need an ice cream freezer. There are many of these on the market, but for this full recipe you will need one that is capable of handling six quarts of ice cream. If you would prefer to make a smaller batch or have a machine that requires it, just adjust the ingredients proportionally down.

Be aware that this ice cream contains raw eggs. If this is something that you object to, you could omit them, but the

flavor, texture, and color of the ice cream might be different. We use our own fresh eggs from the Parris House hens, knowing the conditions that produced them. The other option would be to blend the entire ingredient list and then cook it over low heat, stirring continually, custard style, then chill and then churn.

Lastly, I highly recommend you use real vanilla extract instead of the imitation variety, especially in the ice cream. Because the ice cream is strictly vanilla, without other flavors taking the lead, it's best to use a high-quality vanilla extract for the best tasting result. Likewise, do not use artificial maple syrup, or as our Canadian friends say, "table syrup," in the sundae sauce. These artificial syrups are often made with corn syrup and artificial colors which cannot be trusted to perform the same way in the recipe in terms of flavor and texture.

Bill's Homemade Vanilla Ice Cream

Prep time: **assembly, 15 minutes**

Churn time: **20 minutes or more depending on your machine**

Makes: **Six quarts**

Ingredients

Six eggs

1 cup white sugar

2 tablespoons all-purpose flour

½ pint whipping cream

1 tablespoon real vanilla extract

1 14-ounce can condensed milk

2 quarts half and half

If needed, enough whole milk to fill the rest of your churn container

Rock salt and ice if your churn requires it (does not go in the ice cream!)

Directions

1. Beat the six eggs, sugar, and flour together in one mixing bowl

2. In another mixing bowl, whip the cream in to a soft whipped cream, stirring in the vanilla once it's whipped

3. To the churn container, add the condensed milk, half and half, and the contents of the two mixing bowls

4. If your churn container is not full, add enough whole milk to reach the fill line

5. Churn according to your ice cream maker's instructions

NOTE: If you are using a churn that uses rock salt and ice, it is best to do this outside although here at the Parris House we do have an alternative: we churn ice cream in the antique clawfoot tub upstairs. It may not be ideal for the plumbing to have saltwater running down the tub drain, however, we only make ice cream a few times a year and we flush the drain thoroughly when we are finished. This is also a great solution when the weather outside is unpleasant.

Strawberry-Rhubard-Maple-Syrup Sauce

Prep time: **30 minutes**

Makes: **1 quart plus 1 pint**

Ingredients

3 cups rhubarb, cut into quarter inch to half inch slices

4 cups strawberries, hulled and sliced in halves or thirds

1 tablespoon real vanilla extract

⅔ cup maple syrup

1 teaspoon fresh lemon juice

⅛ cup water

Directions

1. Add the rhubarb, strawberries, and water to a large stock pot and set the stove for medium heat.

2. Simmer this mixture until the rhubarb is tender, stirring occasionally to make sure it is not sticking to the bottom of the pot.

3. Once the fruits in the mix are very soft and starting to blend together, add the maple syrup and lemon juice.

4. Continue to simmer until the sauce cooks down to the consistency of a thin sundae sauce.

5. Remove from heat and store in canning jars in the refrigerator.

This sauce may be served on the ice cream while it's still warm or at room temperature, or you can serve it chilled. If you would like a completely smooth sauce, use a stick blender to remove all of the fruit chunks, but I like the texture of the cooked rhubarb and strawberries.

SUMMER

The Bloom

Summer in Maine should be noted as a bona fide miracle, or at least it feels that way. There are days in July when I look outside at the absolute lushness of the landscape, covered end to end in greenery, vines, blossoms, and wild fruits, and think, "How can this be?" The barrenness of Maine in winter is legendary, and so this phenomenal contrast in a matter of months might make anyone believe in miracles. There is a saying: "No mud, no lotus." It is meant as a life metaphor, and it is without doubt an apt one, but here in Maine, it takes on its very literal meaning. The mud of spring bears the metaphorical lotus – and the literal one on our lakes, rivers, and ponds - in what seems like a million flora and fauna incarnations.

There are wholly unique aspects to summers in Maine, part natural but also part cultural. Maine is known the world over as "Vacationland." In fact, although some of us roll our eyes about it, "Vacationland" is emblazoned on our license plates. If you hear a Mainer use the term "summer complaints," he or she is referring to the massive influx of tourists who visit from around July 4th through Labor Day. I believe many Mainers, myself included, complain much more than is either warranted or even truly meant. For example, the Parris House is not our only home in Maine. We also own an incredibly peace filled century old, fire engine red lake cottage on the western shore of Little Sebago

Lake in Gray. It has been known as "Sunset Haven" since before our stewardship of it began in 2005. Each summer, and the rest of the year, it is the home away from home, as so many of our vacationers describe it, to visitors from all over the country and sometimes Canada and Europe. And so, while it's a summer rite to joke about our tourists, I think many of us would not turn away a single one. OK, well, we wouldn't turn away most.

You do not have to live in Maine, however, to start incorporating more nature into your life during the best outdoor weather of the year, whatever season that might be in your part of the world. You do not even have to be in a rural area. We often travel to cities in our region for weekend getaways and vacations. We go to Portland, Maine regularly and also to Halifax, Nova Scotia, Boston, and other more urban/suburban areas for museums, concerts, and festivals. Without fail, these areas have beautiful natural parks and reserves where anyone could walk for at least an hour or two, get away from the brick and concrete, and practice plant, bird, and animal identification.

At the Parris House, summer means casual meals made with our fresh garden produce sometimes eaten on the screen porch to catch the northwesterly breezes. It means swimming, picnicking, and paddling outings to Sandy Shore, the Pennesseewassee Lake beach area in Norway that's been a recreational spot for Paris Hill residents for about a hundred years. The Town of Paris' public access to the Little Androscoggin River, called the Paris River Park, is open at the foot of our little mountain also. Summer means our 200-year-old windows are open once again 24/7, so that we can hear the old church bell and the train down in the valley more loudly and clearly than at any other time of year. However, it also means a lot of work. Summer is arguably the most labor-intensive time of year at our tiny village homestead.

A typical week at the Parris House in summer includes weeding the garden, harvesting any ripe vegetables, preserving any that are in excess of what we can eat that week, letting the chickens out and collecting the eggs daily, cleaning their coop, tending the bees, including watching for the infamous varroa mite, turning the compost, mowing the lawn, taking our Collie, Wyeth on longer walks and hikes, doing exterior painting, and more. Additionally, the summer volunteer organizations, social and historical, on Paris Hill are in full swing and we are tending to our responsibilities to our community through those.

On top of full-time work commitments outside of homesteading, it's quite a lot to deal with, however usually one bite of a freshly picked tomato or a cool swim at the lake makes it all seem more than worthwhile.

Summer Homesteading

Garden Care

Summer is the most labor-intensive time for the garden. Produce is ripening, herbs are in bonanza-mode, flowers are ready for cutting, and, along with everything else that's flourishing, weeds can be everywhere. This is a time to really pay attention and spend some time daily or near to it in your garden.

Everyone's garden is different, and my purpose here is to give some general tips to beginner gardeners, things I wish I had known during my first attempts at growing my own food.

Keep the Weeds Down

You will never keep them totally out but keep them down. Weeds are more than just a problem of aesthetics. They are

using the nutrients in your soil, encroaching on the growing space of the plants you want, and possibly, in these ways, stunting your garden's development. Unfortunately, there is no one method that completely eradicates weeds in the garden, so we use a combination of approaches that do not include herbicides.

HAND PULLING: This is the method I use most regularly and I think it's unavoidable. Every time I'm in the garden, which is nearly daily at the height of the summer, I pull the weeds I see right off. If you do this regularly it should only take a few minutes and it goes a long way toward keeping the situation under control.

TOOLS: The hoe is my best gardening friend. I run it between rows of plants to uproot the small weeds before they're even large enough to pull and then I rake out the uprooted weed seedlings. There are many other tools on the market for dealing with weeds, but these two extremely basic tools – hoe and small rake – are the ones I use most often.

SEEDLESS, OR NEARLY SEEDLESS, STRAW OR STRAW MULCH: At some point in the season, once all of my plants are well established and beyond the seedling stage, I put straw mulch down between rows or around plants. This does a very good job of keeping the weeds down, looks neat and tidy, and is easy to clean up later or even move around for redistribution if needed. Do not use hay! They are not at all interchangeable. Hay is full of seeds that will create more weeds, not fewer, in your garden.

BLACK LANDSCAPING CLOTH: We only use landscaping cloth at the bottom of the raised beds, under the soil. We do not use it on top to keep weeds at bay. It's very effective if you put it down on the surface of your soil, cut holes for planting, and let only the plants you want come up through. It also can provide warmth and moisture retention to your soil, which is nice particularly in the spring when you want that warmth to become established. I personally do not care for the aesthetics of the cloth, though, and in our case, the raised beds are in the path of a perpetual northwest wind that tends to eventually lift and carry away anything not one hundred percent secured. More generally, it is also harder to add compost or nutrients to your garden after the cloth has been applied. I am even less enthusiastic about black plastic, because unlike the black landscape cloth, it is not biodegradable, not permeable for water to come through, and could, over time, leach chemicals into the soil as it slowly degrades under UV and heat exposure. So, while I can make a very good case for using black landscape cloth in your garden, I can't recommend the black plastic.

Harvest When Ripe

This is another good reason to visit your garden daily or near daily. In the summer you may have vegetables literally ripening in the course of a day. This is particularly true of summer squash, zucchini, peppers, and cucumbers. I have looked at a zucchini at dinner time, opted against harvesting it that evening, and had it grow much larger than I'd wanted in less than twenty-four hours. Most vegetables have a near perfect harvesting time and size and to get the best flavor and texture it's best to pick them promptly.

Keep the Critters Out

This is so important. In my earliest years of gardening I lost so many plants, let alone food later, to groundhogs, raccoons, deer, rabbits, and heaven only knows what other creatures. It's impossibly disheartening. If the animals have not snipped off your seedlings, they will surely forage on your developing vegetables. Here are some options for keeping them away.

LOW POWER ELECTRIC FENCE: As I explained in more detail in the spring homesteading section, this is what we use. Ours is solar powered, is safe for a human or even a small child or pet to touch (although uncomfortable), and so far, has prevented any serious damage to our garden. When shopping for an electric fence, talk to the shop staff to make sure that the power level is both safe and effective.

The methods listed below. have been less effective for us than the electric fence. Each of these methods has proved somewhat effective but still permeable in our particular location, however, might work fine in yours.

ALUMINUM PIE PLATES: String these around your garden on poles or along some kind of fencing. They will move in the wind, catch the sun, and make a little bit of noise, deterring some pests from getting near your garden.

SCARECROWS, PLASTIC OWLS, OR OTHER EFFIGIES: We have a large plastic owl we named Oliver on a pole in the center of our garden and he seems to deter birds from wreaking too much havoc from above. The electric fence will clearly not keep birds out, so Oliver is our somewhat effective attempt. In the past, when our sons were small and loved the project, we also constructed scarecrows with mixed results.

URINE: You can buy animal urine sprays to apply to the perimeter of your garden to repel critters. I am going to confess right here that we never used animal urine, but that there were some under-cover-of-darkness trips out to the perimeter by my husband. We think it helped, but I share this more for your amusement than to recommend the method.

MARIGOLDS AND OTHER REPELLENT PLANTS: I put marigolds in the beds with the vegetables even though I have an electric fence now just because I love the way they look, but they can also be a repellent to rabbits and other small nibblers.

There are so many other methods discussed out in the gardening world for keeping your plants safe, but as I said, I think fencing, particularly electrified, is the most fool proof.

Enrich the Soil

We rotate what we plant in our raised beds and augment the soil each year with new compost prior to planting, but you may notice during the summer that some of your vegetables are not thriving in the way you might have expected. This can be a good time to test your soil again around the specific plants that are not doing as well and get a recommendation for mid-summer augmentation from your local cooperative extension.

Stake, Tie, and Support

I have messed this up on multiple occasions and it goes back to maintaining daily or near daily observation of your garden. Summer is the time when plants start to really take off and mature, so if you have tomatoes that are cageless or growing shoots outside of the cages, beans or peas that will end up on the ground, or large chives/green onions collapsing over on themselves, you need to act. It's so much easier to stake up, cage, or otherwise support plants as they are growing rather than when they are already established to the point where this activity can cause plant breakage and produce loss.

Don't Use Pesticides

Just don't. If you have bees this is particularly important for the health of your colonies, but these chemicals are dangerous to other pollinators in your area as well. We use companion plants in our garden that are known to repel common insects and pests, with good results. These are the ones we have in our raised beds and the best part is that you can also cook with many of these, drying them for preservation during the summer and into the fall. Together, these plants help to stave off cabbage worms/moths, which are the pests most troublesome in our garden, attacking some of my favorite vegetables, including cabbage, broccoli, cauliflower, bok choy, and kale. They keep down other pesky insects too, including discouraging hornworms which, if undeterred, can destroy your tomato crop.

- Marigolds
- Basil
- Dill
- Mint
- Rosemary
- Sage
- Thyme

Be careful with your mint as it is highly invasive. I pull it around its perimeter and use bunches of it in the hen house and nest boxes to repel flies and freshen the air in there.

Get Garden-Sitters

Going on a summer vacation? Get someone to sit your garden almost as vigilantly as they'd sit your pets and livestock. At least every other day your garden sitter should do a little weed control, harvest any vegetables that are ready and store them as you direct, and look for and react to any signs of garden pests. We always tell our chicken and garden sitters that they can take the eggs and produce while we're away, much to their delight, but offering this bonus compensation is between you and your sitters.

Bee Care—Catching that Swarm

Late spring and early summer is when bee colonies are building their populations and may swarm. We try to prevent this, but sometimes our colonies swarm anyway. The good news is that a swarm means your colony is strong! The not-as-good news is that, if you can, you should really catch that swarm.

At the Parris House we have experienced, and caught, multiple swarms. In 2018 we had three swarms and were able to catch two, doubling the size of our apiary from two hives in the beginning of the season to four by the end. Let's talk a little bit about what a swarming hive looks like using an example from our 2018 season.

One weekend, I was working in our garden while my husband was cleaning the chicken coop. Our bee yard is located adjacent to the coop and perhaps a hundred feet from the garden. Suddenly, there was an increasingly loud buzzing coming from the bee yard, which crescendo-ed into a roar. My husband and I shot a look at each other from that hundred-foot distance that said, "Oh no...we know what's about to happen." As I went running toward the bee yard, I could see the bees on one hive already gathering, or "bearding," on its exterior. The "beard" became thicker and thicker as approximately half of that colony and their queen exited the hive. Then, in a breathtaking act of coordination, this

mass of bees, now defined as a swarm, took flight together and left the bee yard, thankfully reperching themselves in a large ball somewhat within reach in our nearby lilac tree. All of this happened in a span of less than five minutes. From first unusual buzzing to balled up in a nearby tree, the span of time was less than five minutes. That is how fast your swarm can exit your hive when it decides it's time to go.

I admit that at that moment my first thought was, "I don't even care if I can catch this swarm; I have just witnessed something extraordinary." A swarming hive is both a spectacular show put on by nature and a very ordinary event in the life cycle of a honeybee colony. This is how honeybee colonies reproduce. For one reason or another, often due to space and resource constraints, the bees will start reducing the size of their normally heavy and flightless queen so that she can fly again and take off with about half the population to find a new home. The half left behind then raise a new queen and one colony becomes two.

So, there we were. My husband and I were standing below the swarm, now about twenty feet up in our lilac, contemplating what to do next. This is why it pays to have extra equipment on hand to house a new colony should one present itself to you, either via a swarm from one of your own hives, or someone else's.

JUST A NOTE:

It is possible to call in more experienced beekeepers to catch your swarm for you. In our area, it is a common courtesy to offer that swarm up to them to keep for their trouble. Many beekeepers are delighted to have a new colony to add to their apiary in this way. As relatively new to beekeeping as I am, I would go out on a swarm call in exchange for another colony. However, I would encourage you to keep your swarm. It's not as difficult to catch one as you may think.

You Will Need

- Your protective bee suit and veil, of course.
- A light-colored blanket or sheet.
- At least one box and set of frames with foundation on them; frames with foundation already drawn out with comb are best if you have them on hand.
- Bottom board, inner cover, outer cover; in other words, the rest of the hive parts.
- Lemongrass essential oil.
- A ladder or otherwise safe way of reaching a swarm if it is high off the ground; should you not be able to safely reach the swarm, consider enlisting help from someone with the proper equipment or abandoning the swarm. No swarm is worth injuring yourself to capture.
- A place in your bee yard to put your new hive.
- You will not necessarily need a smoker during the capture. It is a blessing of nature that swarms are extremely docile. Because the bees have no home to defend while in a swarm situation, they are not very defensive. I have never been stung while catching a swarm. That is not to say that I won't be in the future or that you can't be. You can and should dress accordingly. I am just making this point to hopefully allay some of the natural anxiety most new beekeepers feel when engaged with a swarm for the first time.

Suit up! Always wear protective clothing when working with bees.

Spread your blanket or sheet on the ground directly below the swarm, where you think you are going to place your empty hive. A light color is recommended so that you will be able to see the bees that fall on to it, especially if one of them is the queen.

Place your empty hive, assembled but completely open at the top, directly underneath your swarm if possible. Put a few drops of lemongrass essential oil on to the tops of the frames. This helps attract the bees in.

Before you begin, remember this: once you've shaken the bees down and some are dispersed in and around your new hive, watch where you are stepping! It is not catastrophic to step on a few worker bees during this process. It is much more threatening to the survival of this new colony if you inadvertently kill their queen.

If your swarm is on a branch, take hold of the branch and with one very strong shake, shake the ball of bees down onto/into the waiting hive. Do not be hesitant to give the branch a firm shake. You will not hurt the bees and by having the entire ball fall on to and into the hive in one strong shake, you are more likely to have the queen fall in to the hive as well. This is key.

If the branch is very high in the bush or tree and it is possible to cut it down while still holding the swarm, then gently laying that branch atop the box or shaking them in closer to the box, try that.

You get the idea. In any way possible you want to shake that swarm into the waiting box, as much in one clean shake as you can.

Now watch your bees. This could take a while, but the trend should be for the swarm to be marching into the box. If this is happening, your queen is very likely in there. The bees are responding to her pheromones and following her into their new home. Allow them time to keep moving in. Check on them about every fifteen minutes or so, if you can, to make sure the trend is in. Most of the time, this is the case and searching for the queen is not necessary.

If the trend is not in, it's time to look for the queen. This is where having the blanket or sheet in place can be very helpful. Watching your step, look very carefully in and around the hive and everywhere it is possible that bees from the swarm could have fallen. If your queen is marked, this will be a little easier, but if she is not, just keep in mind that she will not look like the others. However, she has been reduced in size prior to swarming, so do not expect her to be as large as you might be used to seeing queens in a non-swarming hive. Remember that she will have a more elongated abdomen and be somewhat larger still than the workers, shaped differently from the drones. Once you find her, take extreme care to place her into the hive without injuring her. At this point, after a few minutes, you should notice that the bees are all starting to move into the hive.

Once most of the bees have moved into the hive, put the inner and outer covers on and leave it alone for a few hours

while the remaining bees all go in. If you can leave the hive alone until about dusk, you will give most of the bees a chance to go in and will have an easier time moving the hive to its new location. Do not leave the hive in the capture spot too long as you do not want the colony to strongly orient to this location as its new home.

I just want to add a few more notes here about swarm catching. While it is ideal to put your newly caught swarm directly into a hive box, it is not absolutely necessary. In an emergency, you can use some other appropriate box or container for the bees, transport them quickly to a new hive box and location, and install them in that. We just feel that it's probably gentler for the colony if we pop them into their forever home right off the bat, but this is not always possible.

Sometimes swarms are not up trees. Sometimes swarms are on the sides of cars, under patio umbrellas, or on fenceposts. Most beekeepers we know are very creative in scenarios like this. You may need a bee brush in cases like these to gently brush the swarm into your container, being extremely watchful for the queen and working for her protection as wholeheartedly as her colony does.

Finally, if your swarm situation looks like something you truly don't feel confident to handle, quickly call your local bee club, a local beekeeper, or your cooperative extension for assistance. Beekeepers love to assist with swarms. In our area, it is standard protocol to offer the swarm to any beekeeper who comes out to catch it for you, however, sometimes the keeper is just happy to help and you still end up with a brand new colony for growing your apiary.

A Brief Word about Varroa Mites

One benefit of a swarmed hive is that the brood cycle was broken in the process and varroa mites breed in honeybee larvae. Breaking the brood cycle therefore tends to reduce the number of varroa in the hives considerably. What are varroa mites?

Varroa mites are one of the most destructive infestations you can have in your hive if left unchecked. Not only are the mites huge proportionally to the honeybee (akin to you having a tick on your body the size of your fist), but more destructively, they vector viral diseases in the bees. This weakens the colony considerably and colonies going in to fall and winter with a high varroa load rarely survive till spring. A full discussion of varroa is beyond the scope of this beginner's book, but here's a synopsis of what you need to know and explore further with your mentors and local bee club.

In summer, it's important to check your hives for varroa. This can be done with a process known as a "roll." A specified number of bees are removed from the hive, rolled in a jar using either sugar or alcohol, and then the varroa mites that have detached from the process are counted. Counts above the treatment threshold mean the hive must be treated using an effective miticide. Your mentor or beekeeping shop owners can help you decide which treatment is best for your situation.

Please understand that if you have honeybee hives in North America, you will have varroa mites. The only question is how many, so take this threat seriously, test, and treat accordingly.

Composting

We have a continual tug of war at the Parris House between what we decide to put in the compost and what we give as treats to the hens, but even with the hens vying for veggie scraps from the kitchen, we have plenty to compost. Adding mature compost to your garden will provide it with important nutrients and save you from having to buy as much, or any, depending on how much you are able to produce and what your needs are.

Building or Buying a Composter

There are many commercially produced composters on the market and as long as they allow for moisture, aeration, keep animal invaders out, and are large enough to make adequate amounts of compost for your needs, they should be fine. Some require more direct involvement and planning from you than others. For example, there are composters available where all you do is throw the materials in the top, allow decomposition to take place and the smaller bits to filter to the bottom, and then remove that filtered material from a bottom drawer. There are also composters that will do smaller batches in a rotating barrel, but you must turn it daily or almost daily and make sure the moisture content is always adequate for decomposition to take place. There are even composters than enlist the help of worms to break down the material into compost.

As is usual for us, we kept it simpler and cheaper at the Parris House and, being patient and in this for the long haul, we built our own simple, slow process composter out of wood pallets. Wood pallets can often be sourced for free from companies who are disposing of them. Here in Maine, they are sometimes broken up for outdoor firewood, but at

the Parris House we build composters out of them.

This design has a few features many pallet bin plans don't, mainly because we learned that ours need to be predator proof, that I like being able to actually get in to the bin to work it, and that strong and plentiful hinges and handles make a big difference in ease of use.

How to Build a Pallet Compost Bin

To build this super simple pallet compost bin, you will need:
- Five pallets
- Six strong steel hinges
- Four screw-on handles
- Box of long screws
- Chicken wire or hardware cloth
- Wire cutters
- Staple gun
- Power screwdriver
- Power drill

Our compost bins are behind the barn and are not visible from the street. It was never our intention for them to be particularly attractive, so if you have higher aesthetic requirements, this design may not be for your location.

The compost bin has four vertical sides, one of which swings open as a hinged "front door" with a handle. I like this in addition to having just a top entrance because it allows me to open both top and front and literally climb into the compost bin to turn the contents. The top is the fifth pallet, hinged at the back with a handle on the top front. There is no pallet in the bottom. The compost sits directly on the ground.

Before assembly, on the interior of each side, including the lid, staple chicken wire or even finer hardware cloth to keep animal invaders out of the compost.

Now simply screw the pallets together forming a box, only use the steel hinges, three across for each door, for one side on the front and for the top, with the top flipping up from the front. Screw handles, two per door, on to the front and top doors to save your fingers when opening or lifting because, while free and convenient for this purpose, pallets are heavy and awkward to lift.

Jumping off from this simple design, you could also build a double composter so that as you leave compost to continue aging in bin one, you could start new compost in bin two.

What to Compost

It's important to know what and what not to put in your composter. Putting the wrong things in to your composter can lead to pathogens in the finished product, attracting nuisance animals to your yard, or creating compost that will seed your garden with weeds or be too acidic for your plants.

DO COMPOST
- Mostly "brown" materials: leaves, seedless straw, dried grass clippings, small sticks, some shredded paper or cardboard is ok too.
- Some "green" materials: vegetable and fruit scraps, grass clippings, leafy trimmings. The caveat here is to avoid using grass clippings that may have been treated with chemicals. Hopefully you don't use herbicides or pesticides on your lawn.
- Egg shells, preferably crushed a bit to break down more easily
- Coffee grounds, paper filters, and paper tea bags
- Limited amounts of wood ash, however, remember that back in the day wood ash was a component in the making of lye for producing soap. In large enough quantities it could make the pH of your compost too low to be

compatible with your garden plants.

- Nut shells, however, do not use anything – nuts, leaves, branches, or bark – from the black walnut because it contains a chemical that is damaging to plants.

DO *NOT* COMPOST

- Meat scraps. These break down slowly, smell bad, and attract animals. In some communities, however, you can take these to a municipal composting program.
- Plant material containing a lot of seeds, e.g. weeds, grasses that have gone to seed, tomato fruit, straw or hay containing seeds, anything invasive. The seeds can survive and subsequently seed your garden with unwanted plants.
- Manure from carnivorous animals, including your pets. There is a high risk of pathogens and while some of you are probably thinking, "Who would do that?," people do that.
- Commercially made wood mulch. It may be tempting to throw old wood mulch in the composter, but some of these mulches are made from scrap construction materials, contain artificial dyes, or may otherwise contain things you don't want to leach in to your compost and subsequently in to your garden produce.
- Pine needles. These might be ok in limited quantities, but no more than ten percent of your compost, Pine needles are acidic and slow to break down. Too many of these in your compost pile could make the overall pH too low for many plants.
- Coal/charcoal ash from your grill. Coal ash contains a good deal of sulfur, which could be too acidic. Additionally, some charcoal products made for grilling may have been treated with chemicals that do not belong in your compost.

We don't add herbivore manure to your compost. It's a personal choice on our part even though our hen flock produces a great deal of poop/pine shaving mix that, if aged and composted properly, would be perfectly fine – in fact, beneficial – to add to our garden. In our case, we just prefer not to take the extra time required to make sure that manure compost is free of pathogens, is at the right pH and nitrogen level to not burn or damage our plants, and in the right proportion with the rest of our soil. This book is made for beginners and I think that composting non-manure ingredients is a perfectly adequate start. So, what do we do with all of our chicken poop and litter? We offer it up to other gardeners who like working with it.

Turn Your Compost

For your organic material to break down and become rich compost, it requires aeration. Turning compost in a pallet composter is straightforward. I use a wide tooth steel rake and a pitchfork. You can certainly open the front of the composter and turn it while standing at the outer opening, but I put on knee high rubber boots, climb in, and turn it from the inside with the front and top doors open.

Harvesting Your Compost

We were not able to harvest our compost the first year. It just had not yet decomposed enough. As you are turning your compost pile, usually after the first year, you will start to notice a beautiful, finer, dark soil-like compost developing first in the bottom of the composter and increasing in quantity. At some point, with a pallet composter like ours, it's good to stop adding new material to it and let it completely turn to finished compost while building another one to start the process anew. You can then trade off between the two, using the first one up while building new compost in the second, then starting new compost in the first again.

Once you have achieved a finished compost you can work it in to your garden beds in the spring and reap the results of healthier, more robust plants. If you are in doubt about how acidic or what nutrients are in your soil once you have worked in your compost, it's a good idea to get a soil test which can often be done through your local cooperative extension. The test will come back with recommendations for augmenting further if necessary.

Drying Herbs

Summer is the time when the herbs in your garden start to generously multiply, so much so that you may have no idea how to use them all while they're fresh. Basil and mint at the Parris House seem to the be ones we just can't keep up with. You may even find your herbs going to flower or seed before you can use them in cooking. One way to handle this problem is to dry the herbs for later use. Some people like to do this by hanging them upside down in bunches in a clean, cool, dry place, but I prefer the warm oven method because it's quicker and I can efficiently get the herbs stowed in to my pantry for use all through the year. Additionally, with oven drying, I don't have to worry about something going wrong and the herbs molding, accumulating dust, falling prey to household pests, or otherwise deteriorating or losing flavor in the hanging process.

You Will Need

- Freshly cut herbs
- Kitchen scissors or shears
- Colander
- Salad spinner (optional)
- Parchment paper
- Cookie sheets
- Plastic bags, or plastic/glass containers
- Permanent marker

NOTE: You may be surprised and even a little bit disappointed by how much herbs shrink in the drying process. Do not despair. Your herbs are out in the garden all summer growing copiously to be used fresh now and dried later. Plus, freshly dried herbs are potent in flavor and a little bit goes a long way in the fall, winter, and early spring dishes that will follow.

Instructions for Drying Your Herbs

1. Take your kitchen scissors out to the garden and harvest your fresh herbs. Do not cut them all the way down toward the root and do not pull them up by the roots! Harvest the plumpest leaves and stems and leave those still developing for future harvests.

2. If you think there will be a delay in processing the herbs, leave them with their stems in water, up to a day, but it's best to harvest and then process them immediately.

3. If any of your herbs have flowers or seeds on the branches, cut those off. Unless you have another use for them, they are great for composting or giving to your chickens.

4. Remove the most prominent stems as well, anything that would become hard and stick-like in the drying process. It is not necessary to refine the herbs as much as they might be in commercial processing. A bit of stem here or there can either be tolerated in whatever dish the herbs are used in or removed at the time of preparing the recipe.

5. Wash the herbs thoroughly in a colander under cold running water, removing any dirt, insects, debris, or other foreign matter. Another method is to soak them briefly in a pot or clean sink of cold water, scooping them out as they float at the top. This allows all extraneous material to fall to the bottom, leaving the herbs clean.

6. Dry before you oven-dry! I use a salad spinner to remove as much of the washing water as possible and then lay the herbs out on a towel to dry the rest of the way. You could also pat them dry with a clean kitchen towel or paper towels, being careful not to crush them in the process.

7. Set your oven to its lowest setting to get it warm. You want it just warm, not baking.

8. Spread parchment paper on to your cookie sheets, then spread your herbs out on to the parchment paper evenly and with very little, if any, overlap. The idea is for the herbs to dry evenly in the oven.

9. Place the herbs in the oven and prepare to have your kitchen start to smell like Thanksgiving. The herbs will give off lovely aromas as they dry. Check them frequently and remove them when they are the texture of dried herbs: a bit crunchy, leaves crumbling, with no noticeable moisture.

10. Once removed from the oven, you can further de-stem the herbs if you'd like to refine them more. It will be easier now that they're dried.

11. Package the herbs. I have used appropriately sized glass jars, resealable plastic containers, and zip lock bags for storing dried herbs. I do not leave a lot of air in the container with the herbs, so I size the container accordingly.

Paris Hill Founders' Day Celebration

Each summer, on the third Saturday of July, Paris Hill becomes a scene of great celebration for its annual Founders' Day, sponsored by the Hamlin Memorial Library and Museum. The village green is filled with the booths of makers, musicians, food vendors, and local organizations. The Hamlin Memorial Library and Museum is open, as is the Paris Hill Historical Society on nearby Tremont Street. Both organizations have breathtaking artifacts in their collections. It's worth stopping in and speaking with their docents, most of whom live right in the village. The First Baptist Church of Paris, right on the green, allows revelers to ring its nineteenth-century Revere Foundry bell, so the joyful pealing is heard off and on most of the day. Parris House Wool Works, just a short walk north of the green is open for impromptu rug hooking lessons, shopping, and refreshments. Often draft horse and wagon rides are also available for tours of the village.

All of that would seem like enough, but the main attraction is always the world class antique and classic car collection of Bob and Sandra Bahre, whose home is the historic birthplace of Hannibal Hamlin. Just below the home, overlooking the mountains, are state of the art collectors' garages filled with some of the most unusual antique and classic cars you will see anywhere, including museums. The collection features Duesenbergs, a Tucker, Packards, Thomas Flyer, cars of historical significance both in world politics and Hollywood, and more. The curator is always on hand to chat and answer questions. While the car show does have a small entrance fee, all proceeds go to the Hamlin Memorial Library and Museum.

It would be tempting to believe that the Hamlin Memorial Library and Museum is named for Hannibal Hamlin, first vice president to Abraham Lincoln, or that the building was originally connected to the family, but neither is the case. The 1822 granite building that houses the Hamlin Memorial Library and Museum was originally the Oxford County jail.

When the county seat was moved to South Paris because of its proximity to the newly established railroad, county buildings were sold to private owners. Dr. Augustus Choate Hamlin, the nephew of Hannibal Hamlin, purchased the former jail sometime after 1896. It is for him that the library is named. Dr. Hamlin was a distinguished American and Mainer in his own right. He served as the Surgeon General of Maine and also served in high command positions, including Medical Director for the Army of the Potomac during the Civil War. The original deed stipulations put forth by Dr. Hamlin are still honored by the current Board of Trustees and this unique little library and museum are well worth the visit any time of year.

Summer Projects

Scrubby and Soothing Gardeners'
Cold-Process Soap

I don't like wearing gloves in the garden. There, I've said it.

I know they work for a lot of people, thus we have a lucrative garden glove industry around the world. However, I just can't wear them. I've tried.

I don't like not being able to really feel the plants and the earth. There's not enough tactile feedback. Plus, it's almost impossible for me to pull the small weeds with gloves on.

I suppose I do cave in and wear them if I'm handling a hoe or rake, to keep my hands from blistering, but most of the time I come in from the garden with earth-stained hands. As I get older, and just as the gardening season wears on, the earth seems to lodge itself in every wrinkle, nook, cranny, and crack on my hands and fingers. It's not always appropriate to go out in public that way, so this soap is the solution.

Making cold process soap is not complicated, especially with the readily available ingredients we have today. We no longer need to make our own lye with the ash from the hearth, although my sons tried one summer but we never achieved the proper pH. We don't have to render our own beef tallow either. While you may certainly decide to do these things at some point (we have not), I think for beginners it's best to use commercially made ingredients to get the process down, learn all you can about it, and then do any experimenting from there.

We teach a very popular cold process soap making class several times a year at the Parris House and also four classes during the summer at the Sabbathday Lake Shaker Village in New Gloucester, Maine. When I say we, I should really say, my husband, Bill. He is the soap maker at this homestead and he revels in the science and chemistry of it. I'm going to go light with that here in favor of the safety and mechanics of actually making the soap, but a little soap making chemistry is probably important to know.

What Is Soap

Soap is basically a salt, made when you mix an acid with a base. The salt that results from mixing a fatty acid (the oils we will be using) and sodium hydroxide (commonly called lye) has special cleaning properties and is called soap.

How Does Soap Work

Soap works by having a unique molecule that interacts separately with water and oil. One end of the soap molecule is attracted to water, or is hydrophilic. The other end of the soap molecule is hydrophobic, meaning it repels water.

Non-polar compounds, like oil and grease and some sources of stains or dirt, do not dissolve in water. Polar compounds do dissolve in water.

When you add soap to water, as you do when washing your hands, clothing, or anything else, the soap molecules arrange themselves into clusters called micelles. The hydrophilic ends of the soap molecule point outward and the hydrophobic ends, the ends that don't repel non-polar compounds, point inward. These hydrophobic ends at the center attract and trap the oil, grease and dirt at the center of the micelle. With the non-polar compounds contained in this way in the center of the micelle, the water can wash them away.

Soap is also a surfactant, which means it reduces the surface tension of the water it is dissolved in. This also aids in the washing away of oils and dirt.

We are making a cold process soap. Some people understandably get confused about what cold process soap making means, especially given the fact that we do heat the oils to about 100 degrees Fahrenheit when we make the soap. Cold process soaps saponify (turn in to soap) via an exothermic chemical reaction that takes place via the reaction between the fats in the recipe and the lye. You will notice your soap mold actually warming up in the hours after you've poured the soap batter into it as this reaction takes place, followed by a cool down period. It is necessary to allow cold process soap to then "cure" for four to six weeks as the pH of the soap lowers to the right level for skin contact, usually between pH 7 to 10. Lye has a pH of 14 and your soap will be near that when you pour the batter in to the mold, so you really need this aging time to make the soap safe.

Hot process soap, on the other hand, is cooked using an external heat source and is usually safe to use right away, or as soon as it has completely hardened. Hot process soap is often semi-hardened and lumpy when it goes into the mold, so many people prefer the smooth aesthetic of a cold process bar.

This soap recipe is for a completely plant oil-based soap. I like using plant vs animal-based fats because these soaps are suitable for anyone to use, including vegans, and because I have noticed that some animal fat-based soaps can develop an off-odor over time. The cold process we are using in this recipe is also ideal for plant-based soaps.

The soap we are making contains 3 different types of oils that have differing properties: palm oil, coconut oil, and olive oil. Coconut oil produces a very rich lather which helps clean. This alone however produces a softer soap that does not last. In order to make a harder soap we add olive oil. Olive oil however does not always lather well but is improved with the addition of sustainable palm oil. The three together produce a moderately hard bar of soap that lathers well and has good cleaning ability.

So clearly, different oils have different properties. While I am providing a basic soap recipe for you to use here, I would encourage you to explore creating your own. There are many resources online, including calculators for figuring out the proper proportions for any given combination of fats. It is important to note that changing up the oils in your recipe will change the amount of lye that is used in the recipe as well. This is a critical point. Always use a good online calculator or a solid chart in a quality soap-making book to make sure that the lye content in your soap is appropriate to the combination of oils you are using.

Equipment

Do not use anything aluminum or plastic measuring cups. Aluminum is reactive with the lye. Many essential oils will etch anything you have that is the type of plastic used in measuring cups.

- Safety glasses and latex or rubber gloves
- Two-pound latex soap mold with wooden holder, or a glass bread pan
- Food scale that measures in grams and ounces
- Glass measuring cup
- Heat safe stirring utensil
- Stick blender or wire whisk (you're going to want the stick blender, trust me)
- Stainless steel pot
- Rubber spatula
- Candy thermometer or digital probe thermometer, two is best, or you can use an infrared handheld thermometer. In regard to the IR thermometer, I still prefer a thermometer that's actually got a probe contacting the fats or lye.
- Freezer paper
- Large hand or kitchen towel

Safety Precautions

The very first thing we must talk about is safety because we're working with sodium hydroxide (lye) which is extremely caustic. Many of our students are intimidated by this, but with simple safety measures there is nothing to fear. What follows are basic precautions that will keep you safe.

- Always add lye to water, not vice versa. You do not want anything splashing up and on to your skin or into your eyes.
- Mix your lye and distilled water in a well-ventilated area, either outside or in a kitchen or room with an exhaust fan. Do not inhale any vapors that may come off of your mixed lye, or any of the powder that may come off of lye flakes or pellets.
- When mixing your lye pay very careful attention to keeping it in the container. Use a container that's a little big for the job, so that the lye mixture is toward the bottom and fully contained.
- Your lye mixing container should be heat safe, as should your mixing utensil.
- Wear eye protection and protective gloves to keep any inadvertent splatters from contacting your skin.
- Be very careful when you pour your lye into your fats/oils. Again, you want to avoid splashing. Make sure your container is large enough and deep enough.
- Once your soap is at the trace stage, it is still "hot" from a pH standpoint. Do not get your soap "batter" on your skin or in your eyes as you pour it into the molds.
- When cleaning up any utensils or containers that have the uncured soap on them, wear protective gloves.

It is easy to be put off from making cold process soap because of the caustic nature of lye and everything we have

heard about it. However, with reasonable care and a few precautions you will find that it would be very unlikely to receive a lye burn or injury in the small batch soap making process.

Basic Soap Recipe for a Two-Pound Soap Mold

Olive oil - 10.5 ounces

Coconut oil - 6.5 ounces

Palm oil - 4 ounces

Distilled water - 8 ounces

Sodium Hydroxide (Lye) - 84 grams

2-3 tbsp ground pumice, depending on your preferred level of "scrubby"

Essential oils - 1 ounce total, if you are using more than one split them to total 1 ounce

Flowers or herbs - optional, as desired

1. Make sure your mold is prepared prior to starting the mixing processes. If you are using a silicone mold inside of a wooden exterior mold, all you need to do is put any flowers or herbs in the bottom of the silicone mold that you might want as accent on the soap exterior. If you are using a plain wooden mold, you will need to line the mold carefully and tightly with freezer paper. You might also want to do this if using a glass bread pan, but often hardened soap will slip out of a bread pan nicely.

2. Weigh your lye carefully on a digital scale. Follow all safety precautions when handling lye!

3. Weigh your water in a heat safe container.

4. Add your lye to the water stirring constantly, but without splashing, with a heat safe utensil.

5. This mixture will get quite hot before it cools to the temperature you want, so set it aside in a safe place — safely away from pets, children, or a place vulnerable to spilling — until it cools to about 100 degrees. Use your

thermometer to monitor the temperature. If making soap in cool weather, you can accelerate this process by putting your lye outside to cool, but again in a place where no children or creatures can get into it.

6. Weigh out your fats/oils separately on your food scale and then combine them in a stock pot large enough to give you plenty of room for melting and mixing.

7. Melt these oils together over very low heat. You do not in any way want to scald or burn these oils. Bring the oils to just about 100 degrees. Use a thermometer to monitor the heating.

8. When both the oils and the lye are just about 100 degrees, slowly and carefully add the lye mixture to the oils in the soap making pot. You can then start mixing thoroughly by hand, but you will thank yourself a thousand times if you use a stick blender instead. The difference between hand whisking and using a stick blender is about forty-five minutes of labor.

9. You will now start watching for trace. Trace is the point at which the soap leaves - literally - a trace on the surface when you drizzle it over the mixture. It will look like a thick pudding. At this point is has thickened enough to pour into molds but is not too thick to pour. It's very important not to let it become too thick.

10. Just as the soap traces you may add your essential or fragrance oils for scent but do not add the pumice yet! This is also the time to add flowers or herbs you want actually in the soap, as opposed to on the exterior. We encourage you to play with scents, colors, and textures and make your own recipes! Resources online can suggest a variety of combinations, or you can keep it simple with one. Blend thoroughly but quickly so as not to overmix the soap.

11. Just before pouring, stir in the pumice with a spatula or large plastic spoon. You do not want to stir the pumice

in with the stick blender because it is an abrasive and may damage the blades on your blender.

Pour into your prepared soap mold quickly. If there are remnants of soap batter left in the pot that seem to be overtly thickening, don't scrape that into the mold.

12. If you would like flowers or herbs on the top side of the soap also, sprinkle them on now.

13. Cover your mold with freezer paper, wrapping the top like a present, wrap it in a towel, set it aside, and try not to disturb it for 24 hours. It will become increasingly warm as the saponification process further develops, and then it will start to cool again.

Cutting Your Soap

After 24 hours your soap will be completely cool and relatively solid. You still need to wear protective gloves as the soap is still chemically "hot" from a pH standpoint.

Turn your soap out of the mold. If you are using a silicone mold, you should be able to take the silicone part out of the wooden box surround and then gently loosen the sides by pulling on them. Invert the mold on to a cutting surface and gently pull it up and away from the soap loaf.

If you are using a wooden mold with freezer paper, it is very simple. Just take the loaf wrapped in the freezer paper out of the mold and peel away the freezer paper.

If you are using a glass loaf pan, run a sharp knife around the edges of the soap, pop the pan upside down on to a cutting board and very gently tap on the bottom to loosen it out.

With the loaf turned out on the cutting surface, you may use a chef's knife, a wire, or a specially made soap cutter to cut your soap in to the desired sized bars. We usually make our bars around 4 ounces each, or eight equal bars per two-pound loaf, but experiment with yours and cut them to your liking.

Set the bars on to a tray, lined with freezer paper or waxed paper, and set them in a cool, dry place where they can be undisturbed for 4 to 6 weeks to cure. We turn ours every couple of days during the curing process. After 6 weeks your soap should reach a safe pH level for use (we have never had a batch fail to do this), however, testing your batch is highly recommended.

You can use either pH testing strips or phenolphthalein drops that are available from soap supply companies. We use the phenolphthalein drops. Simply put a drop or two of phenolphthalein on to one of your soap bars and observe the color. If the drops are clear or very light pink, your soap is ready to use. If the color is stronger than that, give the soaps a bit more time to cure. Retest in a week.

Hand-Dyed Wool Using Acid Dyes

Dyeing wool for clothing and décor is an activity that goes back thousands of years, and while our ancestors used both plants and sometimes dangerous heavy metals to color their fabrics, this technique uses modern acid dyes.

You can dye wool fabrics and yarns for your own projects quickly and easily. I've been teaching a beginner dye class at the Parris House for several years now and it's always a treat. It's a class that's full of surprises not only for the students, but for me as well. We never know, at the beginning of the class, what variety of colors and textures we'll be looking at by the end of class, and that is by design. While the students are learning specific techniques for creating their hand dyed wools, it is their in-the-moment decisions that determine the colorful outcomes.

We are going to cover two basic methods for acid dyeing wool fabric: pot dyeing and microwave dyeing. There are scores more methods, but these are a great jumping off point for beginners. We are going to be using acid dyes in the following tutorials, which are formulated for animal fiber (wool, silk, alpaca, anything that comes from an animal source).

There are several reasons I have chosen to start you off with acid dyes. One, they are a very easy way for beginners to learn the overall process of dyeing wool. The process does not vary from color to color, the mordants used are the same across colors, and they are readily available. I truly love natural plant dyes, but that knowledge and skill set is more specialized, and I like students to achieve beautiful and somewhat predictable results quickly in the beginning, gaining confidence with the acid dyes and then taking that experience in to natural dyeing afterward.

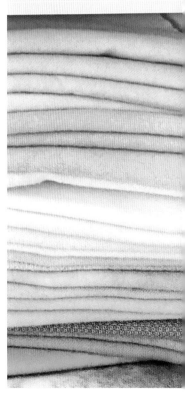

Additionally, acid dyes are very easy to purchase and one brand even has a selection of over one hundred colors to start with. From that one hundred colors, a seemingly infinite palette of colors can be created by combining them into your very own dye recipes, or, if you like, books are available with recipes already created for you. I have to say, though, I prefer my students to experiment with their own recipes because I believe this creates, over time, what feels like an intuitive expertise with the colors, an inner knowing of how to use them and what the results will be when they are combined.

Finally, commercially made acid dyes are replicable, to a point. The recipe you use today should yield a very similar color the next time you use it, assuming your base wool, your water source, and your measurements are all the same. Because this is a hand process, do not expect exact matches batch to batch, but do expect the colors to be close enough to use again in the same or a similar project that you may want to replicate.

There is a simple vocabulary that's helpful to the beginner dyer. Here are some words you may hear or read when further studying dyeing.

- *Primary colors* are red, blue, and yellow. All other colors can be made from these three.
- *Secondary colors* are orange, purple, and green. They are made by combining primary colors as follows:
  red + yellow = orange
  red + blue = purple
  blue + yellow = green
- *Hue* is the discernable color. A piece of wool is red, brown, blue, etc.
- *Value* is the shade of the color from light to dark. It's nice to dye different values of the same color for shading work, or if you want to do a monochromatic piece.
- *Intensity* is the purity of the color; how much or how little of other colors, like black or white or direct

complements, have been added to it. It is often also denoted as how close or not the color is to gray.

- ***Direct complements*** are the colors that are opposite one another on a color wheel. If you add a direct complement to a dye or overdye (overdyeing is putting color over a piece of wool that already has color/is not white or natural), the predominant color will dull or mute. This can also be achieved by adding black to the dye. This technique is sometimes used to make a brighter color more "primitive." Direct complements mixed in more or less equal parts will yield grayish/brownish color.

There are also safety considerations I want to address before we move on to dyeing wool:

- Always wear rubber or latex gloves when handling the dyes. These are chemical dyes that will likely stain your skin on contact.

- If you are sensitive to mild chemical odors you may like to wear a hospital mask while dyeing. Additionally, if you have a kitchen vent/range exhaust vent it would be good to turn it on. Opening windows in nice weather is also an extra precaution. In other words, ventilate as best you can.
- Always use oven mitts or potholders when moving pots of water or dye or working with glass pans in the microwave.
- Wearing old clothing or an apron can help prevent disappointing stains on your clothing.
- If you have granite, marble, Corian, Formica/ laminate, or any other type of conceivably porous countertop in your work area, you may want to lay down plastic to protect it. The dyes *can* stain your countertops. I have caught drips and drops very early on my granite with good success, but I've been lucky.
- Do not use any pots, pans, utensils, measuring spoons, cups, microwave ovens, etc. that you use for dyeing with food later. Your dye equipment must be dedicated to dyeing.
- Even wool that's been out of the dye and resting awaiting rinse can be cool to the touch at the top, but still burning hot in pockets or toward the bottom of the pot it's sitting in. Be very careful when handling wool unless you know for sure it has completely cooled down.
- When using a microwave in the dyeing process, you will be producing trapped steam. Be very, very careful when opening the microwave as steam has the potential to burn you.

Pot Dyeing

Pot dyeing is one of the easiest, most basic ways to dye wool and perfect for a beginner. While the result of the method that follows is a wool of a single color, you do have the option of making that color very solid and even or rather mottling it with darker and lighter areas, all depending on how you treat the wool once it's gone in to the pot.

You Will Need

- Rubber or latex gloves
- Large stock pot or pots, white enamel preferred but not necessary.
- Large white plastic mixing spoons, often available at dollar stores.
- Glass measuring cup
- White vinegar. I buy the gallon size.
- Dyes of your choice. I use mostly Cushing Perfection Dyes. See resource page for more.
- Dye spoons
- Large pot for receiving dyed wool
- Old kitchen towels or rags
- The wool you intend to dye. I recommend dyeing in increments of fat quarter yards.

A NOTE ABOUT DYE SPOONS Dye spoons made specifically for dyeing wool can be expensive and I believe they are unnecessary. You can purchase regular measuring spoons meant for baking, or spoons that are made with increments of "dash, tad, pinch…" inexpensively online or in a culinary or general retail shop. Dye recipes in books may be written

in either the common teaspoon fractions or the alternate. All you need to convert one to the other is this handy chart:

Tad = ¼ teaspoon
Dash = ⅛ teaspoon
Pinch = ¹⁄₁₆ teaspoon
Smidgen (or smidge) = ¹⁄₃₂ teaspoon
Drop = ¹⁄₆₄ teaspoon
And for vinegar as a mordant:
Splash = ¼ cup

Why are we splashing vinegar at all? Vinegar acts as a mordant to the dyes, meaning that it "fixes" them and makes them colorfast and fade resistant. Another mordant in common use with acid dyes is citric acid crystals, available in the canning/preserving aisle of your supermarket. White vinegar is easiest to find, economical to use, and works well.

Directions

1. Start with clean wool that has already been washed. You do not want to dye wool that may have anything from the factory still on its surface.
2. Soak the wool in warm water and, if desired, a tiny amount of dish detergent or synthrapol, which acts as a surfactant, for at least 30 minutes before dyeing. This ensures that the wool is saturated with water all the way through. If it is not, dye uptake may be uneven. It goes directly from the soak to the dye pot.
3. Fill your dye pot with enough water to ensure the amount of wool you are dyeing can be easily stirred. Bring the water to a near boil, but it should not be boiling. The approximate temperature you want is 180 degrees Fahrenheit. I do not use a thermometer, however, you can if you wish.

4. Dip your glass measuring cup into the hot water and bring out the amount needed for your recipe. I usually dye with 1 cup of water, but recipe books may use differing amounts depending on recipe or technique.

5. Mix your dyes thoroughly into the hot water per your recipe or your own combination of colors. Make sure there are no powder clumps left. Even tiny ones can "spot" the fabric.

6. Pour your mixed dye into the pot. Stir very thoroughly to get an even distribution of dye in the water.

7. Now add your wool. It should be transferred right from the soaking pot, fully saturated.

8. If you want a more solid color result, add your splash of vinegar now and stir frequently as the dye is absorbed. If you want more mottling, hold off on the vinegar until later in the process and do not stir as much.

9. As the dye is absorbed the water will become clearer and clearer. Some teachers insist that you must wait until the water is absolutely clear, and others say that you must simmer the wool for about an hour. I personally "dye by eye" and remove the wool when it is in the color range I intended at the value I am looking for, whether the water has cleared completely or not. The risk here is that not

all of the dye, and therefore not 100% of every hue in the mix, has been absorbed, however, if the color is pleasing and the dye is mostly absorbed it will be fine.

10. When the wool looks as you intend, remove it carefully with your plastic spoon (or a spaghetti utensil works well) and put it into a dry pot while you continue your dyeing.

11. When all of your wool is dyed, rinse it thoroughly. I started out doing this by hand in the kitchen sink, letting the water gradually get cooler and cooler as I rinsed. You do not want to shock the wool by rinsing it with cold water if it is still hot, as it can felt. This method is quite a bit of work. It is easier to rinse it in the washing machine. I put it on the hand wash setting, warm, and run it without detergent for a full rinse.

12. The wool can then be dried on low in the dryer or hung to dry.

Microwave Dyeing

Microwave dyeing is a favorite in our classes. If you are fond of tie dyeing, making patterns with color, or just have a great sense of play when you create, you're going to love microwave dyeing wool. Microwave dyeing allows you to use multiple colors on the same piece of wool and therefore creates results that are great for hooking meadows, forest floors, water, and more. If using for applique or other wool craft, these pieces of wool make for colorful and engaging elements.

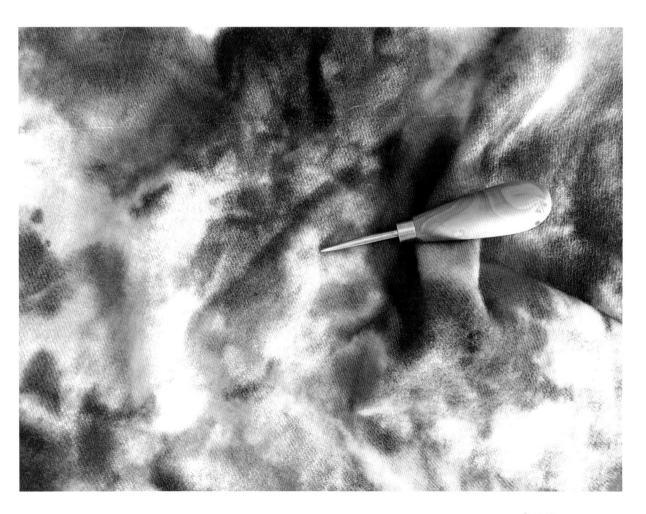

You Will Need

- Microwave dedicated to dyeing; an old one from a yard sale or thrift shop could do
- Rubber or latex gloves
- A 12 x 12 or 9 x 13 glass pan, depending on the size of your microwave
- Dyes of your choice
- Glass measuring cup
- White vinegar
- Dye spoons
- Pot for receiving dyed wool
- Old kitchen towels or rags
- Fat quarter yards of wool. Pieces any larger might be difficult to fit in to your glass pan.

Directions

1. Wash and soak the wool as with pot dyeing.
2. Boil a kettle of water to have on hand for mixing your dyes.
3. You will be mixing your dyes one at a time and pouring them directly on to the wool, but first you must prepare your pan and the wool in it.
4. Splash a little vinegar in the bottom of the glass microwavable pan, about one third to one half cup.
5. Place your wool from the soak pot into the glass microwavable pan. Scrunch! At this point you are going to want to scrunch the wool, making sure that you don't have random corners sticking up or out that will not be covered in dye. Alternatively, you could fan or accordion fold the wool in the bottom of the pan as well, as long as it is spread out in most of the pan.
6. Mix the colors you intend to use one at a time and pour over the wool as directed in step seven. You could

start with three different colors that are either contrasting or coordinating.

7. Pour your dyes directly over the scrunched-up wool in an arrangement that is pleasing to you. This could mean striping, spots, repeats of color, or anything else. I use a fork to move the wool around slightly and make sure there are no spots that are not exposed to the dye. On the other hand, if you would like very light or even white (or undyed) spots in the finished piece, by all means go for it by not poking and prodding it as much.

8. To check that the wool is saturated with dye, peek underneath the glass pan looking for unsaturated or untouched spots on the bottom. If you see any, you can use a utensil to spread the dye a bit more to the underside of the wool.

9. Microwave on high for three minutes. Pull it out, look at it, perhaps poke it around a little more and then microwave for another three minutes.

10. Check to see if the color is mostly absorbed at this point. The water left in the pan should be clear or nearly so. If not, try putting it back in for another minute. IF there are undyed spots in the wool that you did not intend, you can add a little more dye and microwave some more.

11. When the wool is dyed to your liking, allow it to cool a bit and rinse, wash, and dry as with the pot dying method.

Hand-Dyed Wool Using the Simplest Natural Dye: Turmeric

I know some readers will be anxious to try a natural dye, and I'd hate to discourage this so I am including one of the simplest and easiest to obtain dyes for wool: turmeric. I always have turmeric in the pantry because it tastes great, allegedly has health benefits, and it's super pretty on the shelf stored in a Ball jar. I love the sunny yellow of this spice and I think it creates a beautiful hue on the wool. Best of all, turmeric requires no mordanting, which is a bit unusual. One of the factors with natural dyeing that makes it a bit beyond the scope of this book is that mordanting a natural dye is much more complex than mordanting in acid dyeing. Different plants do better with different mordants and some plants will yield different color results depending on which mordants you use with them. Turmeric is more straightforward. No mordanting is required at all. Additionally, even heating a turmeric dye bath is optional. The wool will uptake the yellow over time in a cold soak. That's the good news.

The only bad news is that turmeric is also what is known as a "fugitive dye." This means that over the long haul, the color may not be as colorfast as either acid dyes or other types of natural dyes. Still, if your final product made with this wool is not overexposed to light or is a project where slight fading of the color would not make a huge difference overall, turmeric is a great way to get a gorgeous yellow.

You Will Need

- All of the same equipment as with pot dyeing except the vinegar and acid dyes.
- ½ yard rug hooking wool fabric, cut in to two fat quarters if you wish
- ½ cup turmeric powder

Directions

1. Wash and then soak your wool as with the other methods.

2. Heat the water in your dye pot as with pot dyeing, to just under boiling. Or, alternatively, dye the wool with room temperature water. The uptake of the dye may be a bit slower in unheated water.

3. Add the turmeric powder to the dye pot and stir thoroughly with a wire whisk.

4. Allow the wool to take up the yellow of the turmeric until it reaches a color you are satisfied with. You can leave it in the pot for several hours cooling for maximum absorption.

5. Remove wool from pot and run it through the rinse cycle in your washing machine

6. Line dry or dry in the dryer on low heat

Sunflower Hooked Farmers' Market Tote

Maine is a very strong farmers' market state, ranking high on the locavore scale. This comes as a surprise to many because of our northern climate with its relatively short growing season, but in Maine there are many who have a passion for locally produced foods. I am able to visit at least two farmers' markets, a food co-op, and several restaurants that feature locally grown ingredients, all within five miles of my front door. Of course, this also creates a marketplace for small homesteaders. If we did not have our own shop through which to sell our eggs and honey, we would certainly be able to sell it downtown in the farmers' markets or at the co-op. We keep all of the apples and produce we grow, but if we didn't, markets would exist easily and locally for those too. This is true all over Maine and Northern New England. Why?

I believe there are several factors in play. One, unlike the breadbasket states, we do not have enormous farms here. When New England was settled, creating farmland involved hauling huge granite stones out of the fields before the soil could even be prepared for planting. This is why we are so blessed with ancient and beautiful stone walls at every turn, some maintained by present day owners and some going to ruin in young forests that were fields a century ago. Clearing hundreds of acres was not something that happened in New England. The scale of farming here was and is relatively small. The farms fed their owner families and the local community, especially before the time of quick and easy distribution of food before it could spoil.

A second factor is rooted in more recent history. Maine and New England were a destination for the 1960s through 1980s "back to the land" movement, partially inspired by the work and philosophy of Scott and Helen Nearing earlier in the twentieth century who first settled on a mountain farm in Vermont and then moved their homesteading operations to a saltwater farm in Harborside, Maine. They called it Forest Farm and it is now the site of The Good Life Center, an astonishingly comprehensive educational center and working farm dedicated to homesteading skills and sustainable living.

A third factor is simply this: Mainers have been and remain resourceful people who enjoy interacting with their environment, four seasons out of the year. They are masters of DIY both out of sheer necessity and a healthy pride in accomplishment and independence. This has resulted in small, community agriculture continuing to thrive despite what some might call an "inhospitable" environment.

With all these farmers' markets for shopping, you're going to need a tote! You might as well make it pretty, unique, and durable, literally to last a lifetime. This project fits that criteria. I also intentionally left the background around the sunflowers unhooked so that the linen foundation would show. This keeps the bag light and is a nod to the old-time burlap sacks that were used to transport food and that our hooking ancestors thriftily repurposed as rug backing. Fortunately for you, it also makes this project hook quickly and easily so that in just a few days you might be carrying your tote to the farmers' market.

Please note that the colors listed and shown for this project can be replaced by whatever palette you wish.

You Will Need

- Rug hooking linen, 32" x 20" (you do not need to leave a 4" allowance beyond the size of the bag only because you are not hooking the background, so the unhooked areas serve as your frame allowance)
- 1 fat quarter light yellow rug hooking wool
- 1 fat quarter medium yellow rug hooking wool (I used my turmeric dyed wool)
- 1 fat quarter medium orange rug hooking wool
- 1 fat quarter salmon rug hooking wool
- Rug hooking frame
- Rug hook
- Embroidery scissors
- Coordinating quilting cotton for liner, 33" x 21"

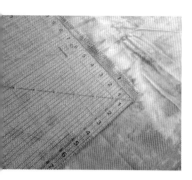

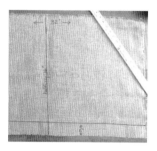

- Coordinating quilting cotton for covering cardboard bottom insert, 9" x 13"
- Heavy cardboard piece for bag bottom, 4" x 12"
- Sewing machine (optional, may hand sew)
- Sunflower tote pattern
- Sharpie
- Ball point pen
- Sewing scissors/shears
- Quilting square
- Matching thread & large sewing needles
- Straight pins
- Heavy utility shears or a box cutter
- White or fabric glue with brush, or fabric grade glue stick
- Handle option: color coordinate cotton twill binding tape
- Color coordinating decorative buttons, 4

Instructions for Cotton Tote Liner

1. Cut a piece of fabric 33" x 21". This gives you a ½" seam allowance so that the resulting liner is the same size as the finished exterior.

2. Fold in half, wrong sides out, and pin the side and bottom together, forming a bag that is approximately 21" x 16.5 inches. One of the 16.5-inch sides will be the open top.

3. Machine or hand stitch the bottom and side seams. One side of the bag will be a fold line instead of a seam. You should now have an approximately 20" x 16" bag. Do not flip right side out.

4. Now make the gusset for the bottom of the bag. Align the side and bottom seam, making a triangular point. Pin in place.

5. Using your quilting square, with the 45-degree angle

line, measure a 4" bottom gusset, 2" on each side of the seam. Mark the 4" line with a pen and pin on either side of the line, leaving room for your sewing machine if you are not hand sewing.

6. On the other side of the bag you will have only the bottom seam and the fold line. Match the fold line and bottom seam up just as you matched the side and bottom seam on the other side.

7. Mark the 4" bottom gusset on that side as well.

8. Stitch directly on your 4" bottom gusset lines.

9. Leaving about a half inch, snip off the corners beyond the seams. Do not snip before the seams or you will have holes in the bottom of your bag! You will now have a nice rectangular gusset on the bottom of the bag.

10. Do not flip right side out. This liner is going to slip right into your hooked exterior with the wrong side against the wrong side of the exterior, the right side of the liner forming the nice finished interior of the bag.

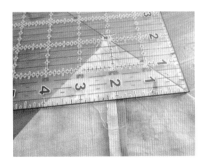
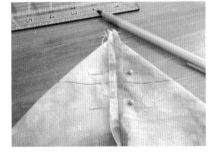

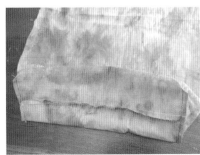
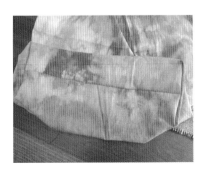

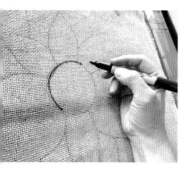

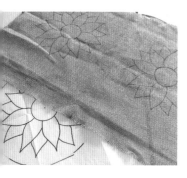

Instructions for Hooked Exterior of Tote

1. Cut a piece of linen 32" x 20". You do not need to leave a frame allowance as with most hooked projects. This is because for this project you are not hooking a background. Therefore, you will have plenty of bare linen around your design to keep it on the frame.

2. On the 32" side, measure up 2" from the bottom and, using your Sharpie, draw a line straight across, keeping the Sharpie in the grain of the linen. This is just a reference point for where the gusset fold is going to be on each side of the bag and will help you center the design where you want it.

3. Draw a line vertically at 16" down the center, bisecting the 32" side. This is going to serve as a reference for where the side fold in the bag will be and will also help you place your design on each side of the bag. Note that all of these markings are on the wrong/interior side of the pattern and are just used as reference points.

4. Using these reference points as a guide, perhaps making tiny marks on the right side of the linen just at the very edges of the pattern where the bag will be sewn together, trace your sunflowers on the right side of the linen, one centered on what will be each side of the finished bag. You can pin the paper pattern in place under each side before you draw. Be sure to take into consideration the two inches of gusset area at the bottom of each side and raise the design up to be centered accordingly.

5. Once you have the sunflowers drawn on to the pattern, you can serge or zigzag the edges of the linen so that they do not ravel while you are hooking. Do the serging or zigzagging on the very edge of the linen so as not to lose any length or width as these are the actual edges of your bag.

6. Hook your sunflowers! (See basic hooking instructions in the Spring section of this book.) I recommend using at least three colors on each petal and a single color in the center. When you hook the petals make sure that you are using contrasting colors where the petals come together so as to define them one from another.

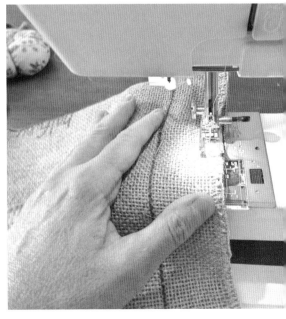

7. (Optional) I like to clip the loops in half in the round center of the sunflower creating a shaggy texture that differentiates it from the smooth loops on the petals. Just take your snip scissors, put them through the center of each loop and snip the loop in to two equal "tails."

8. When you are finished hooking the sunflowers, steam and block them. (See instructions for steaming and blocking in the Spring section of this book.)

9. Now it's time to assemble the exterior of the bag. Just as with the liner, fold in half and pin with wrong sides out. Machine or hand sew the side and bottom of the bag. Because you are working with linen that has wide holes, I recommend sewing these seams at least twice.

10. Make the gusset using the same method you used for the liner. Once this step is complete DO turn this part of the bag right side out.

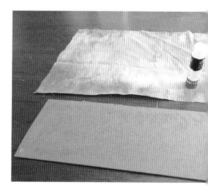

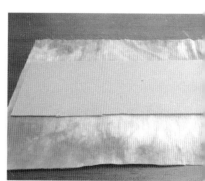

Instructions for the Cardboard Bottom Insert

1. Using heavy utility scissors (not your fabric shears!) or a box cutter (please be careful!) cut a 4" x 12" piece of heavy cardboard. The thick cardboard that bolt fabric is stored on works well. If you do not have an empty bolt cardboard center around your home, I'd bet your local fabric shop would give you one.

2. Take your 9" x 13" piece of coordinating quilting cotton and practice wrapping the cardboard with it like a gift.

3. Once you are comfortable with how you are going to wrap the cardboard, brush glue or better, use a heavy-duty fabric glue stick, on to the cardboard and adhere the fabric to the cardboard neatly, with your folds on the bottom. You may weight this with a book or books until the glue dries, or if using the glue stick, it will dry almost immediately.

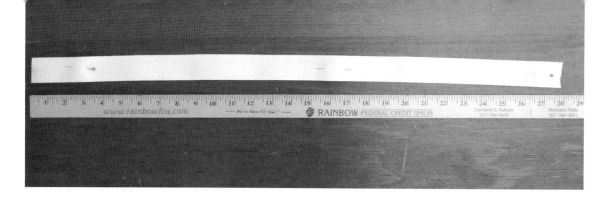

Tote Handles

You have a lot of different options for these. First, decide whether you'd like to carry your tote on your shoulder or carry it by hand, the way a typical reusable grocery bag is carried. This will determine the length of your handles.

There are many wonderful handles available, in cloth, leather, vinyl, and other materials available at your local sewing or craft shops. Readymade handles can make this project even simpler and will also allow you to choose from a wide variety of lengths.

For my tote, I stuck with the rug hooking theme and chose to use cotton twill tape rug binding for the handles. I did double the thickness of the tape by sewing two pieces together using a simple straight stitch in a contrasting color. The length of my handles, prior to attachment, is 24 inches, giving me enough room to carry the tote on my shoulder.

Assembly of Exterior and Liner with Handles

1. You're going to stitch the exterior and interior liner together at the very top edge of the bag, so place the liner into the bag so that its right side is the side you see when you open the bag.

2. Carefully fold in the edges of the linen exterior and the cotton liner toward one another, about half an inch, and pin in place.

3. At this same time, position the handles so that the

ends that will be attached to the bag are sandwiched between the exterior and interior liner. I positioned mine about 6.5 inches apart, inside to inside of the handle. Leave at least an inch of the twill tape handle end sticking down between the exterior and liner. Pin the handle attachment points in place.

4. Start hand stitching the exterior to the liner. I used a simple overhand stitch with the stitches showing to maintain a rustic/primitive look, however you have options here. You could machine stitch this part, or you could use a decorative blanket or other embroidery stitch around the upper edge to add an embellishment. The only non-negotiable considerations are that you have the correct sides of the exterior and liner showing and that the handle attachment points are securely sewn.

5. To reinforce the strength of the handle attachment points, sew decorative buttons to the exterior of the bag at each point, sewing completely through all layers of fabric.

6. Put the cloth covered cardboard insert into the bottom of the bag and you're ready for the farmers' market, the beach, or anywhere you'd like to show it off!

Heritage Skills for Contemporary Living

Summer Recipes

Summer is all about fresh produce! If you are gardening, it's about letting your ripening fruits and vegetables guide your menu planning. If you are part of a CSA (Community Supported Agriculture) or a patron of the local farmers' market, you can still enjoy planning your meals around what is newly and freshly available at every point in the season. The abundance of fresh food in summer creates a fun challenge to try new things and get out of the menu rut many of us find ourselves in at other times of the year.

As I've mentioned, I'm a transplant to Maine who had never seriously grown even an indoor pot of basil prior to coming here, but I had Italian grandparents in Drexel Hill, Pennsylvania, just outside of Philadelphia. My grandfather, who arrived as a boy in America via Ellis Island circa 1910, was a master tailor, gardener, and wine maker. He grew things few people grew in southeastern, suburban Pennsylvania, including large Italian squashes, figs, and wine grapes. My grandmother dutifully took the produce and turned them in to pure magic. While I do not recall my grandmother actually making the heirloom tomato & basil pie offered to you here, it is my own twenty first century homage to my grandparents' amazing growing and cooking skills, nonetheless.

The recipes that follow are meant to take full advantage of the summer season, here in Maine and in your neighborhood too. The prominent ingredients are fresh garden greens, usually available all summer in a wide variety, luscious tomatoes, farm fresh eggs, and fresh cheese available at most farmers' markets if you are not making your own.

Garden Fritatta

Prep time: **10 minutes**

Cook time: **10-15 minutes**

Serves: **4**

Frittatas are the ultimate easy summer meal. They are fast to prepare and adaptable to just about any combination of meats and vegetables you have in the house. This frittata uses a combination of vegetables we have from the Parris House garden every summer that I think combine well for an interesting flavor and texture, but you can use anything you have on hand. If you're hesitant to fire up the oven on a particularly hot day, cut the milk back to 1/8 to 1/4 cup and the cheese back to ½ cup and combine these ingredients stove top for an omelet instead.

Ingredients

1 tablespoon olive oil
6 eggs
½ cup whole milk
1 cup shredded cheddar, gruyere, or relatively hard cheese
    of your choice
¾ cup zucchini, diced
10 cherry tomatoes, seeds removed, halved
1 large banana pepper, seeds removed, sliced
¾ cup kale, shredded
1 sprig fresh dill, main stems removed, the rest chopped
Salt and pepper to taste

Directions

1. Heat oven to 400 degrees Fahrenheit
2. Whisk eggs, milk, salt, and pepper together until well blended, set aside.
3. Heat the olive oil in a 10" iron skillet on the stove top and make sure the entire surface of the pan, including up the sides, is coated with oil. Add a little more if needed.

4. Toss the vegetables into the olive oil and sauté until just slightly softened. I like the veggies to still have a little body and crunch to them in the finished frittata. To achieve this, it's best to toss the kale in a little bit after the rest of the vegetables.

5. Remove the skillet from the heat, arrange the vegetables evenly in the bottom of the pan with a spatula, and sprinkle the cheese in evenly on top.

6. Pour the egg mixture on top, making sure that it's evenly distributed in the pan.

7. Sprinkle the chopped dill on top.

8. Bake for 12 - 18 minutes until the center of the frittata is firm and does not run when poked with a sharp knife. Our big vintage Wolf range runs a little on the cool side, so we cook it longer, but the knife test works well no matter how your oven runs.

9. Allow to cool for at least 5 - 10 minutes to give it time to firm up a bit and then slice into wedges.

Heritage Skills for Contemporary Living

Italian Grandma's Heirloom Tomato Pie with Farmers' Market Cheeses

This is a very hearty pie and can be a full dinner by itself or served with a light Italian style salad and a crisp wine.

    If you'd like to make this with a thinner crust it would make it lighter and keep the tomato, basil, and cheeses the unequivocal stars of the show, but many Americans are used to a thicker crust so that's the way I have made this one. If you do go with a thinner crust, also slice the tomatoes and cheeses thinner and keep a close eye on it so that it does not burn.

Prep time: **20 minutes**

Cook time: **20 minutes**

Serves: **8**

Ingredients

Pizza dough, homemade or store bought

Simple tomato sauce (see recipe with separate ingredients below)

3 tbsp olive oil and 1 tbsp balsamic vinegar, whisked together

Fresh basil

3 – 4 fresh tomatoes in a variety of sizes and colors, sliced thin with seeds and juices around seeds removed

1 pound fresh mozzarella, sliced thin

8 ounces herbed chevre

¼ cup grated asiago

Optional: 1 tbsp balsamic vinegar and 3 tablespoons olive oil, whisked together, for drizzling over the finished pizza after baking

    You may substitute the tomatoes shown for any kind you are growing or are available at your farmers' market or grocery store. You may also substitute the fresh mozzarella and asiago for cheeses of your choice.

Simple Tomato Sauce

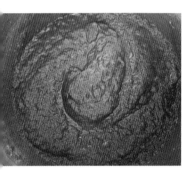

1 tablespoon olive oil

3 cloves garlic, crushed then minced

1 – 28 ounce can crushed tomatoes

1 – 10 ounce can tomato paste

Pinch salt or to taste

Directions for Making the Sauce

1. Heat the olive oil in a saucepan and sauté the garlic in it until soft and fragrant.
2. Add the crushed tomatoes and blend well with the oil and garlic.
3. Allow to simmer for five to ten minutes as the sauce absorbs the flavor of the garlic.
4. Add the tomato paste to thicken, stir and heat through, then add salt to your preference.

This recipe is going to make more sauce than you need for the pizza, but I like extra every time I make sauce so that I can either use it in other recipes the same week or pop it in the freezer for later.

If you wanted to take a little more time with this step, you could cook your own tomatoes down and substitute them for the ready-made crushed tomatoes. Just be sure if you use this method that your tomatoes are scalded, then peeled and de-seeded prior to cooking them down.

Directions for Making the Pizza

1. Preheat oven to 425 degrees Fahrenheit
2. Spray a 14 to 16-inch pizza pan or stone with cooking spray or wipe it down with a thin layer of olive oil. For

additional anti-sticking properties, you could also
sprinkle it with cornmeal after oiling.

3. Spread your pizza crust thinly on the pan or stone.
4. Spread the sauce thinly and evenly on the dough.
5. Lay on the fresh mozzarella slices to cover the pie.
6. Lay and overlap the different types of sliced tomatoes
on to the pie, alternating them evenly around the pie to

cover it, then crumble on the herbed chevre.

7. Intersperse fresh basil leaves with the tomatoes to your taste preference. Basil is a strong herb so use only as much as you like.

8. Sprinkle the grated asiago on top.

9. Bake for about fifteen minutes, then check the pie. You are looking for the crust to be baked but not burned, the tomatoes to be heated through, and the cheeses to be thoroughly melted. Watch the pie for up to ten minutes more until it meets these criteria. If the crust is browning too much before the tomatoes and cheeses have warmed and melted, reduce the heat in the oven for the remaining cook time.

10. When completed, drizzle balsamic/olive oil mixture over the pie if desired. Enjoy!

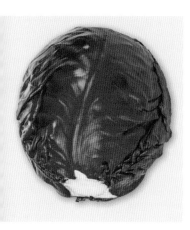

Home-Fermented Sauerkraut

Late summer in Maine is when our garden cabbages, carefully watched over for most of the season, become ready for harvest. We often grow red or purple cabbages, just because we like the colorful results in our recipes, but you can use any color you like for fermented sauerkraut.

I chose sauerkraut as the fermented recipe for this book because it is among the simplest to do and most of us know intuitively how sauerkraut should look, smell, and taste. It is therefore easy to gauge its progress in the fermenter and contrary to the fears of many newbie fermenters, it's very difficult to get it wrong. It's also a great recipe for serving with red hot dogs (this is Maine and our hot dogs are red) for end-of-summer Labor Day celebrations.

I like things to be easy, so I have a dedicated fermenting jar with an air-lock lid and ceramic weights to keep the vegetables below the brine line. The jar is 3-liters, so it's large enough to make good sized batches of vegetables that can then be stored in the refrigerator when the desired level of fermentation has been reached. Fermented vegetables will continue to ferment a little bit once transferred to the refrigerator, but not nearly as rapidly as they do at room temperature in your fermenter. It is likely that your refrigerated final product will not change dramatically in the time between refrigeration and consumption.

I kept this recipe completely straightforward in case this is your first attempt at fermenting. I did not add garlic, peppercorns, or other seasonings because I think it's a good idea to ferment a vegetable straight up to discover its unembellished taste and then move on to experimenting with flavoring it in future batches.

A word about fermentation and how it works. The process by which we ferment vegetables is called lacto-fermentation.

This is because the active bacteria in the process is lacto-bacillus, which is a bacteria that contributes to healthy gut flora and fortunately can survive in high salt environments. Remember that we ferment vegetables in a brine solution. Most bacteria that can be harmful to us cannot survive in a brine solution and are killed off early in the process. Then, the lactobacillus takes over and converts the sugars in the vegetables into lactic acid, which is what gives our fermented food both its preservation and its tasty tang. Lactic acid is literally the preservative that makes fermented foods safe to eat, flavorful, and nutritious. The longer this process continues, the more lactic acid is produced and the tangier the food becomes. This is why it's good to assess your vegetables each time you ferment and decide how you'd like to adjust time on the next batch, should you like them a little tangier.

You Will Need

- Fermenting equipment. We use the Kilner glass jar fermenting set, but you can use any glass canning jar with weights and an air-lock lid. For this recipe a half

gallon sized canning jar would be a good size.

- 1 medium head of cabbage sliced thin. I used half red and half green.
- 1.5 – 2.5 tablespoons sea salt. Do not use refined salts or salt with iodine.

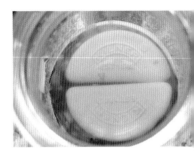

If you need additional brine, as explained below, make it with 1.5 tablespoons sea salt per quart in unchlorinated water. Never use chlorinated water in a fermented food because it can inhibit the process.

Directions

1. Put your sliced cabbage in to a large bowl and sprinkle it with the salt.

2. With clean hands and/or a large, firm spoon, "muddle" the cabbage. Press it, squeeze``` it, and compress it until the natural juices come out of it. This can take ten minutes or more so please be patient. Ideally, you will get enough juices from the cabbage so that when you pack it in to the jar it is completely submerged.

3. Pack the cabbage in to the jar, pressing down to try to submerge it in its own juices.

4. If you do not have enough of the cabbage's juices to submerge it, you may augment it with sea salt made with 1.5 tablespoons brine to 1-quart unchlorinated water. Only add enough brine to submerge the cabbage completely, perhaps by about an inch.

5. Once you have the cabbage packed and submerged, place your weights on top of it to keep it from floating up.

6. Put the airlock lid on your fermenter jar.

7. Place the fermenter jar in a warm but not hot place, ideally around 65 degrees, but the temperature can range as low as 55 to as high as 75. The rate of fermentation increases in higher temperatures. We are not able to tightly control this on the pantry shelf where we place our jar and yet we have not had any problems.

8. Allow your sauerkraut to ferment for 2 to 4 weeks. The higher the temperature during fermentation, the faster the fermentation takes place. Also, the longer the food ferments, the tangier the flavor, so if you like your sauerkraut tart, let it go more toward 6 weeks.

After fermentation is complete, open the jar and transfer the sauerkraut to jars in your refrigerator. It will keep in the refrigerator for up to three months and the flavor may continue to develop.

Many people new to fermentation are concerned about

their fermented foods "going bad" in the fermentation process. As I mentioned before, this is extremely rare. When you open your jar for the first time, there should be a fresh, pickle-like smell, the sauerkraut should not be slimy or mushy, and it should also not be darkly discolored.

Signs of a truly bad and unsafe ferment are a foul smell and/or a black or very dark mold growing on or in the food. If you smell or see either of those, throw the batch away. Some people are also ok with a white mold growing just on the surface of their fermented foods, but I have to tell you, I'm not. If I were to see mold of any color, I'd also throw the batch away. I realize this makes me less than "hard core" about fermenting, but I am in the better safe than sorry camp on this. Fortunately, the vast majority of the time you will neither see nor smell anything amiss. Your fermented food will be fresh, healthy, and tasty.

FALL

Color and Texture

Fall is my favorite time of year in Maine. It is wickedly unpredictable and the older I get the more I appreciate that aspect of it. Will there be high color or not so much? Will it be 70 degrees or 30? Will the leaves gently rustle in the breeze or will they be stripped from the trees in a nor'easter? Or maybe, as occasionally happens, just to be contrarian, the wind will come from the southwest, warm in my face. It may be tee shirt weather on Halloween in Maine, or there may be snow on the ground. I remember one particularly fierce Halloween with very low temperatures and high winds. Most of the hundreds of Trick or Treaters we get through the historic village were undeterred, however, my youngest son, then only about four, was not having it and we headed home. The next year was spring-like.

This wild variability is one reason why you must be flexible in the fall here to get all your fall homesteading activities done. It's almost impossible to stick to a firm schedule that's consistent year after year. Fall homesteading is more of an art, where you are reading your plants, observing your livestock, and paying close attention to the weather reports, which, in New England, are good for about five minutes. About the only thing that is consistent during the fall is that the days are shortening and so it seems there is even less time to get everything done.

Another reason that fall is my favorite time of year is that it provides a visual and textural bonanza of inspiration for any artist, including textile artists. New England is famous for its fall foliage season and visitors from all over the world start arriving usually in late September to enjoy the spectacle of the turning leaves. In my village, visitors also like to walk or drive slowly by the historic homes, taking in the architecture and sometimes trying to steal a peek into the windows. When I first arrived in Maine, this felt a bit like an imposition, but I have gotten used to it and remember a time when I might have been tempted as well. It is no wonder that art inspired by Maine and New England often features motifs of leaves, trees, farmland, and mountain and seaside villages.

Much of my fall textile art inspiration comes from my daily walks with my Rough Collie, Wyeth. We leave the Parris House and head north, away from the village and down the road past the large open field that belongs with one of the most historic homes in our area, Old Brick. Built in 1813, Old Brick is a three-story brick Federal that still looks much like it would have when it was new. It was built by Captain Samuel Rawson and his wife, Polla. They had at least three daughters, Frances, Arabella, and Columbia, who were all raised at Old Brick. Columbia married Virgil D. Parris and they purchased the Parris House in 1853. Descendants of Samuel and Polla Rawson are the stewards of Old Brick to this day. What inspires me most on my walks, however, is their field. The field is a four season, endless source of visual inspiration and is no less beautiful in the fall than at any other time of year.

Old Brick's field has an unimpeded view of the White Mountains, including Mount Washington, which are ablaze in color right around October. The first snows of the season generally "stick" to the highest elevations but melt at the lower ones. Mount Washington stands at 6,288 feet, while Paris Hill is at only 820 feet. As a result, we get to see the

White Mountains turn true-to-their-name-white somewhat early in the fall as snow covers their peaks. This results in a spectacular view from the field, color contrasted with the snowcapped peaks, and one Wyeth and I enjoy every single day on his walks in fall. Or perhaps I am the one enjoying the view while Wyeth is busily sniffing his way along the ground. Closer to his eyes are the crunchy leaves on the ground in a plethora of shapes, sizes, textures, and colors and the bittersweet, invasive but breathtakingly beautiful, reddening on the vine.

While not as busy as summer, fall is a still an active time of winding down and buttoning up at the Parris House. We are still harvesting our small garden and canning, freezing, and drying everything we cannot use immediately. The apples must be picked before they fall to the ground or are eaten by deer and tree-climbing porcupines. They also must be preserved. The beehives must be evaluated for their fitness going into winter, including an assessment of how much honey to leave for the bees and how much we might extract for ourselves. Wood needs to be cut and stacked. The hens typically slow down on their egg production as the days shorten and likewise, we also seem prone to shortening our productive hours as darkness falls increasingly earlier.

Heritage Skills for Contemporary Living

Fall Homesteading

Harvesting Honey

Harvesting our honey is one of the most rewarding yet messy fall activities at the Parris House. We extract on the westerly facing screen porch because this is a task that cannot be done in the open outdoors. Extracting outdoors is prohibited because you will soon have honeybees, and possibly other insects, clamoring to get a taste of your harvest. As it is, we see our bees occasionally buzzing outside the screen, keenly interested in what we're doing. So, if you are extracting, find a good spot indoors that you can also reasonably clean before and after harvesting. Cleaning before is just a good food safety practice. Cleaning after is, well, a necessity as it is impossible to keep all that sticky honey one hundred percent contained during the process.

Honey extractors come in a variety of sizes and capacities. We only have four hives at the Parris House and have not, to date, taken off more than one hundred twenty pounds of honey at a time. We are small scale, meeting our own needs and selling our extra. Since we are not doing a large amount of extracting, we can get by with a small, hand cranked extractor. Additionally, we have only recently purchased a good quality, used extractor. You may want to wait also. There are modestly sized extractors with all of the necessary accessories available for around $500 or less, but we think we benefitted by waiting.

We are still growing our apiary and still don't know how large it will be in future years or how much honey we'll be harvesting. So far, we have only extracted honey in the fall and have reserved a great deal of honey for overwintering our hives. Weather in Maine is extremely unpredictable. A turn toward dry, early dearth conditions can stunt honey production later in the season and so some years you may save all of your honey for your winter hives instead of harvesting. These uncertainties slowed our decision to purchase an extractor and when we did purchase, it was mainly because one came on to the market used at a price we could not resist.

If you do not want to purchase an extractor right away, it is often possible to rent or borrow an extractor and all the necessary equipment very inexpensively for your small homestead sized harvesting. While this sometimes means waiting for the equipment to be available from your local beekeeping shop or club, it saves you from purchasing and storing the equipment yourself. This could be a particularly convenient option for those of you without large garages, barns, or other storage space. If you are unsure of whether or not this is an option in your area, contact your local beekeeping club and ask.

NOTE: If you are selling your honey, check with your state Department of Agriculture and/or Cooperative Extension about any food processing licensing or labeling regulations that may apply. We have a State of Maine food processing license and our kitchen has been state inspected and certified so that we can bottle and sell our honey here. We also have bottle labels custom printed with all of the information required by state law. These regulations vary by state, so just make sure you are in compliance if you wish to sell your harvest!

With all of that said, let's show you how extraction is done!

You Will Need

- Your full honey supers/frames
- Uncapping knife
- Uncapping rake

- Extractor
- Multiple large buckets, preferably at least one with a closeable outlet valve
- Fine sieve/strainer
- Drop cloths or tarps
- Enclosed space; this is never done outside in the open! Your bees will know if you are extracting in the open and they will attend the party.
- Clean jars and lids
- Jar labels (optional, but likely needed if selling your honey)

Step 1 – Prepare your space

- Cover everything! Seriously, cover your surfaces. We use a large blue tarp to cover our porch floor and make sure that any furniture is well out of range or covered also. You may also want to have a pair of slip on/slip off shoes or boots so that if you have to leave the extraction area you are not inadvertently tracking honey into other areas. It's just messy, especially if you are a beginner and this book is primarily written for…beginners.

- Lay out everything you need in the space before you begin and do so in the way that makes the most sense to you, within easy reach and according to the order you will need those tools.
- If you are using an electrically heated knife to uncap the honey, make sure you have a safe place to plug it

in and a heat proof surface on which to lay it down. I cannot emphasize this enough. These get hot. You must be careful not to burn yourself or anything in your environment. Arrange the cord in a way that will not tangle or get in your way or accidentally flip the knife on to you or the wrong surface. Always be very aware and intentional when handling a heated uncapping knife.

- Have your honey supers full of honey frames in the space with you so you do not have to keep going into another area for them. If you had any of your supers stored in the freezer, make sure that they are completely thawed before you extract the frames.

- Have a large enough bucket for your cappings. You'll be able to get wax from these later. Make sure it is large enough that you will not be dripping (much) honey over the side of it as you uncap your frames.

- Have plenty of space around your extractor so that you are not backed into a corner trying to use it. Depending on what kind of extractor you have and how well balanced it is, you may want a second person to help stabilize it while it's being cranked. If this is the case, you especially need to have enough space for both of you to comfortably fit around the extractor.

- Have at least a five-gallon bucket at the output of your extractor with a mesh sieve fitted in to the top for filtering. You're going to have pieces of wax and possibly a few bee parts in the honey as it comes out of the extractor. The fine mesh sieve will filter all of that out. You will be surprised at how much honey comes out of a frame and how fast that bucket can fill.

Step 2 – Load the Extractor and Spin

NOTE: Take a look at your honey frames before you extract them. Are all the cells capped or are there some areas of

the frame that have uncapped honey/nectar in them? This is important because you do not want to extract frames with a lot of uncapped honey on them. Uncapped honey has a higher moisture content than capped honey and having too large a proportion of uncapped honey in your batch can lead to fermentation. While mead is a great adult beverage, that's not what we're aiming for here.

- It is very important that your extractor is loaded in a balanced way. Because it works by spinning at high speeds, like a centrifuge, if the frames are not in balance in terms of number and weight, the extractor will not spin smoothly and not extract as well. Think of a washing machine off balance.

- Your frames will need to be loaded in one direction, spun, then loaded in the reverse direction and spun again.

- Make sure all of the safety features on the extractor are in place. Many extractors have lids not only to keep the honey from spraying up and out in a fine, sticky mist but also to ensure that no one gets an extremity in the way of the rapidly spinning frames and the metal brackets holding them. Extractors also

Heritage Skills for Contemporary Living

sometimes have safety features on the cranks so that you have to be intentional about engaging the spin mechanism before it will start rotating.

- Spin! Whether this means starting an electric motor or turning the crank yourself, start the process. Within a minute or so you will have honey starting to pool in the bottom of the extractor barrel.
- Reverse the frames and spin again.
- Repeat this process until you have extracted all of your honey frames.

Step 3 – Filter the Honey

- Most people like to eat filtered honey, free of any unidentified particulate. Fortunately, this does not require anything more than having a fine sieve in place as the honey comes from the extractor into your bottling bucket. We do nothing more to the honey than this filtering. We do not pasteurize it or otherwise heat it and therefore we sell it as raw honey. Honey is naturally antimicrobial and will not spoil in its raw state. Pasteurizing compromises honey's delicate flavors, which vary delightfully based on what the bees have as forage, and its nutritional value.

NOTE: Raw honey should not be consumed by infants under one year of age or persons with compromised immune systems because it is rare, but possible, that raw honey can contain the spores of clostridium botulinum. These spores cannot reproduce in raw honey, but it is believed that if consumed by these populations they can grow in immature or compromised digestive tracts. As always, it is best to be safe and not feed raw honey to infants or immunosuppressed individuals.

Step 4—Bottle the Honey

NOTE: We bottle in glass. We like to use glass because it is reusable, recyclable, and sustainable. Sometimes our honey customers return the bottles to us for reuse, which is nice but not necessary. We do buy the classic pear shaped, ribbed sides, one-pound honey jars, however you can certainly just use canning jars which are often a little less expensive.

- Wash and/or sterilize your jars. Technically, it is not necessary to sterilize the jars because honey is naturally antimicrobial, however, we do it anyway just as one more squeaky-clean precaution. We just run them through the sterilize and heat dry cycles in the dishwasher.

- Just as with extracting, prepare your space! I put a large towel on the floor underneath the honey bucket and tap. Then I figure out where the tap is most likely to drip just a tiny bit and put a clean bowl on the floor in that spot, on top of the towel. This way drips are caught and the spilled honey can even be reclaimed for our own use.

- Grab your clean jar and put it under the honey tap with one hand. Open the tap just enough for the honey to come out at a rate you can manage. If it comes out too fast you're likely to have a very sticky mess all over the jar, your hands, and the floor. I do not use a funnel. If you manage the tap opening a funnel is not necessary.

- Fill each jar in this manner! Screw the lids on as you go and you're all set to enjoy your honey or give it away as gifts. If you are selling your honey, label the jars in accordance with your state regulations.

Step 5 – Clean the extractor and all of your equipment

Clean your extractor and your equipment in cold water. This is very important. It is tempting to clean the equipment in hot water, because it is natural to think that this will help the honey flow off the surfaces. However, honey is very water soluble and will clean off perfectly well in cold water. So why not warm or hot? Well, you're also going to have some wax residue in that equipment from the frames and cappings…

If you use warm or hot water that wax will melt and spread itself all over the interior of the extractor and all over your tools. At that point, it is quite difficult to remove. So, remember, cold water only.

Garden Clean-up

I recommend not procrastinating in the garden clean-up chore. I had to learn this lesson the hard way during a recent season.

I travel to Nova Scotia several times a year for both personal and professional reasons. We have friends and family there and it's like a second home for me. So, one fall I decided to leave for Nova Scotia the first week of November and stay up there for about ten days, visiting people and spending focused time on some work projects. I had not yet done my fall garden clean up, but I figured there'd be at least a few weeks when I returned to get the job finished.

I was wrong.

I returned to Maine to find a fresh blanket of new snow on the ground, one that did not melt away until the following May. I ended up doing my "fall garden clean up" in the spring, which is less than ideal. It adds one more significant chore to the already task-heavy spring homesteading calendar.

Garden clean up need not be complicated, though, especially with raised beds. Here's what I do.

- Remove the last of the fall produce if there is any left. These are often the pumpkins and winter squashes, although kale and even tomatoes can go quite late in to fall too. Sometimes this means you'll have a pretty big stash of food to preserve all at once, so factor that in to the schedule this time of year.
- Remove any support structures, for example, tomato cages, bean poles, or any other extras you had in the garden for the plants. Especially if you had any trouble with plant diseases during the season, clean these

items before you put them away. If you have fencing, remove it now.

- Clear all the dead or dying plants, including any weeds. Pull any plants that are annuals and have withered or just stopped producing. These will be all of the vegetables but if you have a floral and herb bee garden, like we do, leave the perennials alone. If the pulled plants were healthy, you can compost them. If they were diseased in any way, they should be disposed of, but not in your compost bin.

- You can add a layer of compost at this time and then cover the beds with a thick layer of straw mulch. I tamp the mulch down a bit because in our location, wind is an issue and can possibly carry some of it away.

One option that can be nice for the wildlife is to do this clean up in two steps, days apart. I often harvest the vegetables, take the fence, tomato cages, and support structures down, and then walk away for a few days. Before long I am watching wild turkeys, deer, and sometimes other creatures gleaning what's left in the garden. When they've taken what they can, I go back to finish the job.

Freezing the Apple Harvest

Every other year at the Parris House we have more apples than we can possibly use as a family. As you'll see in the fall recipes section, we do cook some down into applesauce, but we also freeze some for later use in pies, cakes, and other recipes. It's simple and easy and recipes taste just as good as if you'd used freshly picked apples.

We have a hand cranked apple peeler/corer, but you don't need something this all-in-one to do this job. Simply peel the apples your preferred way, cut the flesh off the core and then slice the apples to the desired thickness. I do find that if I slice them a little thicker than I would if using them fresh they are firmer after freezing.

Weigh out 2-pound allotments of peeled apple slices. This amount makes a nice 9-inch apple pie later and it is not necessary to defrost the apples before baking.

Place the 2-pounds of apple slices into a gallon resealable freezer bag and close the bag all the way except for a tiny bit at one end through which you can insert a drinking straw. Using the straw, suck all of the excess air out of the bag and quickly seal. This is an inexpensive alternative to a vacuum sealing unit, however, if you have one this would be an excellent time to use it.

Label the bags with the month and year, pop them into your freezer, and use the apples all the way through to the next apple season in whatever recipes you wish.

If you are freezing apples specifically for pies, here's a fun alternative.

Instead of freezing the apples plain, toss them in ½ to ¾ cup sugar, ¼ cup all-purpose flour, and 1-1/2 teaspoons cinnamon prior to bagging. Place the coated apples in the freezer bag, remove as much air as possible, but this time don't just place the bags in the freezer. Take your pie plates, put the bags in to them, shaping them closely to the interior of the plates, and freeze in the shape of the plates. You can remove the pie plates from the freezer after the apples have frozen into shape.

When you go to make pies later, just remove the plastic bag, set the already sugared, and spiced frozen apples into the bottom crust, add a little butter on top, put on the top crust, and bake as usual. It takes longer to bake a pie using frozen apples, but just keep an eye on it. You will know that it is done when the interior is bubbly and hot (you can use a temperature probe to determine this) and the top crust looks finished. Because you are baking a little bit longer, you may want to use foil or an aluminum crust protector around the edges of the top crust.

I have had apples prepared this way keep in the freezer for two years, however, I recommend just planning on one.

Halloween on Paris Hill

Halloween on Paris Hill is something we start preparing for about six weeks in advance—or whenever the Halloween candy appears in our local supermarkets. We buy a few bags of candy at a time, rather than buying it and hauling it all home in one go. This is because we get hundreds of children trick-or-treating in our village every year. In rural Maine, neighborhoods with sidewalks, closely spaced homes, and good street lighting are not the norm. So parents bring their kids to trick-or-treat in our neighborhood.

Some Paris Hill residents go all out for Halloween and decorate their antique homes in the spookiest of ways, much to the delight, and occasional fright, of the children.

At the Parris House, we have a crock-pot tradition each Halloween night. Rather than trying to cook while darting back and forth to serve trick-or-treaters, we make a simple meal with a crock-pot of meatballs for sandwiches and one of mulled cider. Often there is also a salad, pumpkin pie, and maybe some cupcakes. For us, this is the official start of the fall holiday season and we get to share it and our beautiful neighborhood with families from far and wide.

Making and Freezing Pureed Pumpkin and Roasting Pumpkin Seeds

We do not have much land here at the Parris House, so as a result we do not grow a lot of crops that take up vast amounts of space. This includes pumpkins. However, I can rarely resist growing at least one plant so that we have some fresh pumpkin grown on our own land. Yes, pumpkins from serious growers are plentiful and relatively cheap here in Maine every fall, but I enjoy watching our pumpkins develop from their beautiful yellow blossoms right on through to the mature vegetable. There's something very cheerful about watching pumpkins ripen as the days get shorter and the air gets colder.

Aside from the lack of a large growing space, I also refrain from growing a lot of pumpkins because processing them can be a fair amount of work. You need to be dedicated to that, and to eating, or giving away or selling, a lot of pumpkin the rest of the year, if you want to grow a large number of them. So, for us, one or two plants is plenty. As the vines grow, they also provide a nice cover for parts of our garden space we'd ordinarily have to weed, mow, or otherwise keep clear. I just make sure that I keep training the plant to the area I want it to cover, not letting it shade anything else in the garden I don't want to inadvertently impede.

We'll cover two types of freezer preservation here, one using pumpkin and one using a large heirloom variety winter squash called New England cheese squash. These methods will work for any type of good sized, hard fleshed winter squashes, including common varieties like butternut and acorn. Because pumpkin is often used mashed or pureed in breads, pies, and soups, we'll use that for the pre-cooked method that follows first.

Freezing Pre-Cooked Mashed/Pureed Pumpkin

STEP 1 – ROASTING YOUR PUMPKIN

- Be sure to wash your pumpkin thoroughly after harvesting it from the garden or bringing it home from your local grower or grocery store. Pat it dry and cut it in to two halves, vertically, from stem to bottom.
- Scoop out the seeds and set aside. These will become a delicious snack! When you scoop make sure you really get all of the stringy innards out so that none remain in the halves you are about to roast.
- Line a roasting pan or cookie sheet with sides (the pan must have sides to catch any moisture that bakes out) with aluminum foil and place the pumpkin halves skin side up on to the pan or sheet.
- Put the pumpkin halves in to the oven at 350F and check them every half hour for softness. It should not take more than an hour or so for the pumpkin to roast, but times vary with different ovens. The pumpkin is ready to remove from the oven when you can pierce it easily with a fork, the skin is starting to brown in places and become soft, and you could easily mash the interior with a potato masher.

NOTE: Do not overcook. If you overcook the pumpkin it can become a little watery. This is not the end of the world. It can be drained if this happens, however, it is best to catch it sooner.

Once done, remove the pumpkin halves from the oven and set them aside to cool. They are way too hot to handle at this stage but leave the oven on.

While your pumpkin is in the oven and/or while it is cooling, you can be preparing the seeds.

STEP 2 - PREPARING YOUR PUMPKIN SEEDS FOR NEXT YEAR'S PLANTING (AND FOR HEALTHY SNACKING)

- Rinse the seeds carefully in a strainer and remove all of the leftover pumpkin flesh and stringy material from them. Do not throw this away! Set all of the leftovers aside in a bowl to be either composted or given to your chickens. The Parris House hens love pumpkin and squash processing days and come running as soon as they see me with the scrap bowl.

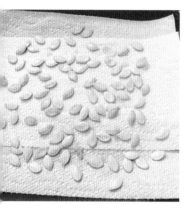

- Once the seeds are separated out, take some subset of them out for planting next year. Set them out to dry on a cookie sheet lined with a couple of paper towels. Let them dry completely, up to a week, away from heat, moisture, and mice (it happens). When they are completely dry, package them in a dry jar or paper envelope for planting in next year's garden. Save a few more seeds than you want in case they do not all germinate.
- The rest of the seeds are yours for healthy snacking! Pumpkin seeds are an excellent source of fiber, potassium, and magnesium. They are high in fat and therefore pack a lot of calories, but eaten in moderation they are a wonderful, crunchy snack by themselves or as an additive to breads, granolas, and trail mixes.

- Make sure your pumpkin seeds for roasting are relatively dry. Spread them on to a kitchen towel and either pat all remaining moisture off of them or roll them up in the towel and squeeze gently. When you unroll the towel they should be almost dry to the touch.
- Spread your dry pumpkin seeds out on a cookie sheet

and add a teaspoon of the oil of your choice. I like to use olive oil, but avocado oil is a nice alternative. Toss the seeds and oil around until the seeds are well coated and will not stick to the cookie sheet. Add sea salt if desired or any other seasoning you especially like. I like the pumpkin seeds with savory seasonings vs spices, but experiment and have fun with adding flavors.

- Roast the pumpkin seeds in the oven at 350F until they start to brown a little bit. Check them every 5-10 minutes. You can let them brown slightly, toss them around a bit with a small spatula, and let them brown some more, but do not overbrown. They should be crunchy, but not burned.

- Once roasted to the desired doneness, pull the seeds out of the oven and let them cool while you're doing the next step of the pumpkin processing.

STEP 3 - MASHING/PUREEING THE PUMPKIN AND PACKAGING FOR FREEZING

- Scoop all of the soft flesh out of your roasted pumpkins and set it in to a colander to drain just in case it is watery. Moisture level varies according to type of pumpkin or if the pumpkin became slightly overcooked. You can press down on the pumpkin gently to get any excess moisture out of it during this stage.
- When drained, transfer the pumpkin to a bowl. Using a hand masher, cranked food mill, a stick blender, an electric blender, or a food processor, mash or puree your pumpkin to the desired consistency. Especially if you are using it for pies or breads, you might want to get it fully pureed.
- Once mashed/pureed measure out two cups of pumpkin and put it in to quart size freezer bags. I use two cup increments because this is the amount of pumpkin I generally use in a standard sized pie.

NOTE: You ***must*** use freezer bags, ***not*** regular plastic storage bags. Freezer bags are designed to keep food fresh longer in the freezer than regular storage bags and are usually made of a heavier plastic. If you object to using plastic for food storage, you may also use appropriately sized jars, leaving some room for expansion, however you do not want to leave much room because any air left in the jar invites freezer burn and a shorter storage life for your food.

- Be sure to get as much air as possible out of the food storage bag. I lay my bags flat and allow the puree to settle flat in the bag, then push the air from the top as I am sealing. If you have a vacuum sealer, you are all set on this step.
- Mark your bags with the content name and the date.

If I'm freezing something I only process once a year, I know I can just put the year on the bag, however, if it's something I'm processing several times a year, I put the month or season and the year on the bag.

- Freeze! A nice option is to lay your bags flat on a cookie sheet in that flat, airtight configuration. It not only helps with keeping the pumpkin fresh longer, it's very space saving to stack the bags in the freezer compactly when they are frozen this way.

STEP 4 – FINISHING AND STORING YOUR ROASTED PUMPKIN SEEDS

- Make sure your seeds are completely cool, then pat any excess oil off of them with paper towels. When you have completed this step they should not leave an oily residue on your fingers.
- Roasted pumpkin seeds can then be stored in glass jars, plastic containers, or a decorative fall covered dish. Just keep them away from moisture and, if not eating them all right away, in a cool, dark place.

Freezing Winter Squash in Whole Pieces

If time is of the essence, here's a faster way to process and preserve your winter squash or pumpkin. This method can also be used for other fresh garden produce such as peppers, celery, cherry tomatoes, and more.

STEP 1 – CUT UP YOUR SQUASH
- This is the time to make sure you have a very sharp knife and a firm surface. Wash your squash thoroughly and cut it vertically, from stem to bottom, in half. Scoop out all of the seeds and stringy insides and save them for your compost or chickens. Cut the halves again in to quarters and then you may cut again in to eighths depending on the size of your squash and how small you'd like your pieces. I end up with pieces that are about 2" x 2". Take the long slices that result and cut in to manageably sized chunks. Then take a paring knife and cut off the rind, which you may also compost or feed to your hens. You should now have skinless chunks of firm, raw squash.

STEP 2 – LAY SQUASH CHUNKS ON A LINED BAKING SHEET
- Line a baking sheet that fits in to your freezer with waxed or parchment paper. Place your squash chunks on to the sheet so that they are not touching. Repeat this on as many pans as necessary.

STEP 3 – FREEZE!

- Carefully lay the baking sheets flat in the freezer and allow the chunks to freeze in place. Do not remove them until they are completely frozen. It is not necessary to cover them. This is super simple; just freeze them right on the sheet uncovered.

STEP 4 – BAG AND LABEL

- Once frozen, take the chunks and package them in to freezer bags, labeling each bag with the content and date. You might want to use a food or postal scale to weigh out equal portions, perhaps a pound per bag, for easier use in recipes. Place back in the freezer.

NOTE: For some people, the simplest way to preserve a pumpkin or winter squash is simply to put it whole in a very dry, very cool place like a root cellar or an attic and just retrieve it when it is about to be used. I do not use this method for several reasons. One, I think freezing is a much more controlled method. I know the food will not spoil because of an unexpected condition in my storage area and I can also keep it safe from, as well as not attracting, mice or insects. Two, I believe freezing at the point of harvest keeps the food tasting fresher. Three, I love the convenience of taking premeasured amounts out of my freezer for immediate use in recipes without having delayed the processing aspect until I actually need the ingredient. Having said all of that, if you'd like to try the cold, dry storage method with your pumpkins or squashes, by all means do so. Just carefully inspect your produce at the time you go to use it for any signs of spoilage or infestation. Chances are, there will not be any trouble, but it's always best to be on the lookout for any food safety issues when you store food in that way.

Saving and Ripening Green Tomatoes

Here in Maine, our tomato plants often keep producing right up to the first freeze. If you have plants loaded with green tomatoes that will never have time left to ripen on the vine, you can still save them and ripen them indoors. Here's a simple method that works well if you have a cool, dark, dry place to store them and that can provide ripe red tomatoes well in to the holiday season and beyond.

You will need

- Bleach
- Newspaper
- Cardboard boxes

STEP 1 – WASH YOUR TOMATOES

- Wash any surface dirt from your tomatoes and remove stems and leaves. Look for any open cracks, holes, or obvious signs of damage or decay. Discard damaged tomatoes or try ripening them on the windowsill, watching for spoilage, but do not attempt long storage with those.
- Fill the sink or a large pot with cold water. Add just a little bleach, approximately 10%, or 1 part bleach to

9 parts water. Dip your tomatoes in this solution and then rinse thoroughly with cold water.

- Let your tomatoes dry completely on a clean towel or gently pat them dry.

STEP 2 – WRAP AND PACK

- Once completely dry, wrap each tomato individually in a piece of newspaper. Pack these loosely into a cardboard box, no more than two layers deep.
- Close the box and store in a cool, dry place, ideally a basement or root cellar where the tomatoes will not be disturbed by any pests.
- Check tomatoes for ripening every five days to a week or so. Remove any tomatoes that show signs of decay and promptly use those that are ripe.

NOTE: Some people put an apple in with the tomatoes in order for the apple's natural output of ethylene gas to speed ripening. I do not do this, preferring not to risk an accelerated ripening of the tomatoes, however, it is a perfectly viable practice.

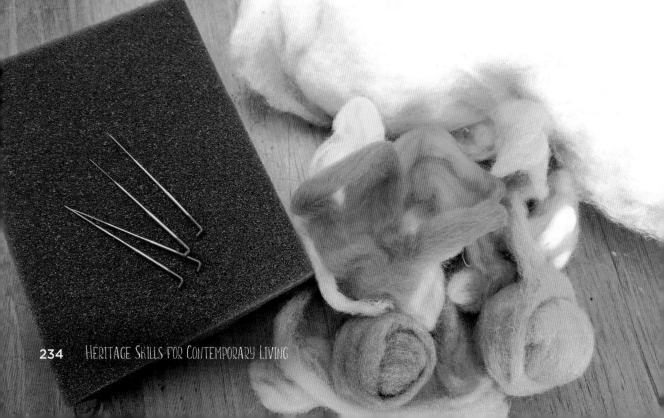

Fall Projects

Needle Felted Apples & Pumpkins with Hand-Dyed Roving

Needle felting three dimensional objects is like sculpting with wool. The process takes a blob of fluffy, abstract wool roving and turns it in to a relatively solid, representational work of art. You can felt wool in to anything: animals, plants, fruits and vegetables, fictional characters, whatever you can imagine. In this project we are going to start with easily made apples and pumpkins to celebrate the arrival of fall and add to your fall decorating options.

You Will Need

- About 1 ounce wool roving for each main color, either in light neutral colors or already dyed in red and orange. You will find that a single ounce of wool roving is quite a bit of roving!

- About ½ ounce wool roving for any accent colors you'd like to use, meaning colors felted over the main color, or any color used to make leaves and stems. I used an accent orange for the pumpkin, an accent mauve for the apple, an accent brown for the stems, and two greens for the leaves.
- If dyeing your roving, acid dyes made for dyeing wools, protective plastic gloves, and white vinegar
- Felting needles – 36 gauge for coarse work, 38 gauge for general use, 40 gauge for fine work
- Foam felting block

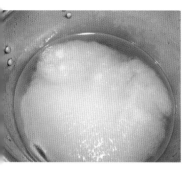

Dyeing Roving with Acid Dyes

Dyeing roving is very similar to dyeing wool fabric, as we did in the Spring section. There are some differences since it is more fragile when wet than wool fabric, especially if you are using smaller pieces for the purposes of this project. If you wish to move right on to the felting, simply purchase your roving already dyed. Check the resources section of this book for great options for buying pre-dyed roving.

1. Wear protective gloves for this process.
2. Soak the roving in warm water. Add a splash of white vinegar to pre-mordant it.
3. Heat another pot of water on the stove until just under boiling.
4. In a measuring cup, mix 1 cup of the hot water with ½ teaspoon of the acid dye of your choice. Mix thoroughly until there are no clumps or dots of dye left in the cup.
5. Pour the dye and water mix in to the pot of hot water and stir thoroughly.
6. Immerse your roving in the dye and allow the color to develop to the desired shade. Ideally, when all the dye is taken up the water will clear.
7. When the roving is dyed to the color you want, gently and carefully remove it from the pot with a slotted spoon, wide plastic tongs, catching most of it in the tongs, or a spaghetti server. Place the hot roving in a clean bowl or pot to cool.
8. When the roving is cool enough to handle, rinse it under warm running water until it no longer smells like vinegar and the water running out of it is clear.
9. I dry my roving by gently laying it out on a dry towel, not stretching it in any way. Once it is thoroughly dry it's ready for felting.
10. Repeat for each desired color.

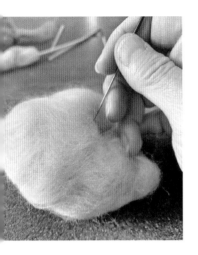

Needle Felting Apples and Pumpkins

I think the most important part of this process is an initial safety warning, especially if you are doing this project with children. Always make sure that your fingers or hands are not in the path of the needle. I don't think it's possible to get seriously injured in a needle felting mishap, but I do think getting poked by a sharp felting needle can be discouraging and for younger children, put them off from felting for a while. In the case of two dimensional flat felting, it's harder to hurt yourself because your project is lying flat on a foam felting block, but in the case of felting 3D objects, we are sometimes holding and turning that object with our hands while it is developing, so attentiveness is essential.

In needle felting, the barbs on the end of the needles work to condense and adhere the roving to itself and/or to another felted object. The wool fibers entangle as the barbed needle hits them and by this mechanism you are able to sculpt the wool roving in to anything you like. The more refined the detail you are trying to achieve, the finer the felting needle you should use. For example, you might start a project with the coarser needle and end up with the finest one for finishing details.

1. Take a ball of roving at least two to three times the size of the object you want to make, in the color you want to make it, and gently tear it from the larger piece of roving.

2. While carefully avoiding hitting your fingers or hands and using the felting block as a base upon which to set your project, start stabbing the ball of roving with your felting needle in quick, sharp stabs, working it gradually into the shape you desire. It's best to have a felting block to set it on as you work, but you also might be picking it up and felting it in your hands at times, so be careful! You will be turning the piece and refining the shape as you work. This truly is a sculpting process, with moment to moment refinements made as you work just as though the material were clay or stone.

3. For the pumpkin, you might felt in the vertical ridges once you have the general shape established. For the apple, you might felt in the stem area and bottom indentation, top and bottom, the same way.

4. As you felt, the piece will become denser and tighter. If the piece becomes too small, simply add more roving and continue to shape and felt it in to the size desired.

5. Once you have the basic piece established, you can add highlight colors and accents using other colors of roving. You can also add stems and leaves by felting these smaller objects on the foam felting block and then felt-attaching them to the larger object via a similar stabbing motion.

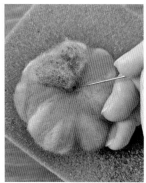

The piece is finished when you are content with the way it looks and there are not lots of obvious wispy pieces of roving hanging out of or off of it. It should be a compact, three dimensional object ready to display in your fall décor or give as a gift to someone you love.

Beeswax Lip Balm

Lip balm is a must for me in the fall and this easy-to-make, beeswax and honey lip balm is a sweet reminder of how industrious the bees have been the previous summer. If you have melted down and purified your own beeswax, good for you! However, if you do not keep bees or prefer not through that process, it is very easy to find beeswax pellets for sale that can be used in this recipe as well.

You will need

- Microwave or double boiler
- Lip balm tubes, small lip balm jars, or lip balm tins
- If using lip balm tubes, it's handy to have a lip balm tube filling tray and spatula

Recipe

3 tablespoons beeswax, grated, chopped, or in pellets
2 tablespoon shea butter
3 tablespoons coconut oil
½ teaspoon sunflower oil
2 teaspoons honey
¼ teaspoon vitamin e oil

OPTIONAL: Add 10 drops of your favorite flavor oil of your choice to this recipe.

Makes about ½ cup or 16 lip balm tubes. The recipe can be scaled down if you want to make less.

Directions

1. If using lip balm tubes, assemble them underneath the lip balm filling tray, open ends up and forming the support of the tray.

2. Put all ingredients in to a double boiler until well melted or you can carefully use the low/defrost setting on your microwave to melt them. Do not scorch or overheat the wax and oils. They should be just warm enough to melt together.

3. Once all ingredients are melted, whisk them together until well blended. If you are using a flavor oil, add it at this time.

4. Carefully pour the warm lip balm in to the containers. If using the lip balm tube filling tray, use the accompanying spatula to get all of the balm in to the tubes.

Honey and Goat Milk Body Butter

Fall is the time in Maine when my skin starts needing extra TLC. It's not uncommon to start heating the house with both wood and heating oil as early as September and this creates a dryer than usual environment. Additionally, fall chores and activities tend to be tough on the hands, so having a moisturizer that both works well and helps to seal moisture into your skin is helpful.

This body butter works so well, especially on heels, elbows, and chapped hands, that I make a pretty large batch and then store the extras in a cool place until I'm ready to use them. While this recipe is shelf stable for months, I do not have an overt preservative in it and so keeping it in the refrigerator just makes it last a little longer. I also give it away as gifts in pretty mesh or burlap bags with gift tags on.

This recipe makes eight four-ounce jars. If you do not want to make this much body butter at once, just scale the recipe back.

You Will Need

- Stand mixer
- Measuring spoons
- Food scale
- Bowls for measuring out the oils
- Rubber spatula
- Screw top glass storage jars or small resealable plastic tubs, your choice of size. I use 4-ounce glass jars that come with little spatulas, which are convenient and also more sanitary than putting your fingers in the jar with each use.

Ingredients

16 ounces shea butter, cut in to small pieces
5 ounces coconut oil, melted
1 tablespoon goat milk powder
1 tablespoon honey
¼ teaspoon vitamin e oil
1 tablespoon skin-safe essential oil of your choice.

> My favorites for this recipe are lavender or Valencia orange.

NOTE: This recipe can be made unscented also if you wish, or the essential oil scaled back to your preference.

Directions

1. Weigh out five ounces of coconut oil, melt it until soft and runny and put it into your stand mixer bowl.

2. Weigh out sixteen ounces of shea butter, cut it in to small pieces, and add to the mixer bowl.
3. Whip this combination until it is smooth and fluffy.
4. While adding the next ingredients, use a spatula to push any body butter than creeps up the sides back down into the bowl so that everything is thoroughly mixed.
5. Add the goat milk powder and honey, then whip again.
6. Add the essential oil and whip thoroughly a final time.
7. Pack into clean jars or plastic containers and store in a cool place.

Paris Hill Hook In

Each November since 2013, we have hosted the Paris Hill Hook-In at the historic First Baptist Church of Paris on the village green. While this event includes no more than sixty guests each year, it has an established following now in the regional North American rug-hooking community.

Hook-ins are an integral aspect of rug hooking. A hook-in is a gathering of rug hookers, each bringing his or her projects to the event. The events usually span most of the day, but the most popular hours are 9 a.m. to about 3 p.m., allowing those who have traveled a distance plenty of time to get home before dark. Door prizes and giveaways add to the festive atmosphere and there are often brief educational segments and demonstrations.

These events are very common in the epicenters of North American rug hooking, which are New England and the Canadian Maritimes. This is where rug hooking was invented and where it remains relatively strong. As you move out from this area, both in the United States and Canada, the art becomes less and less well known. However, there are very good resources for finding hook-ins occurring all over the continent. These are *Rug Hooking Magazine's* online event calendar, the Association of Traditional Hooking Artists (ATHA) list, and the online group, Rug Hooking Daily.

At the nineteenth century First Baptist Church of Paris, there is not space to have more than sixty attendees, and, as it is, our attendees are split in to the "front room" and the "back room" of the church's basement. I also only have room for three rug-hooking supply and goody vendors. In addition to myself, usually in attendance are the inimitable Cherylyn Brubaker of Hooked Treasures in Brunswick, Maine, and Ellen Skea Marshall of Two Cats and Dog Hooking of Bethel, Maine. So why do I use this venue year after year and why does the event always sell out?

It's the soul of it. It's the way the venue helps us to remember who we are and where we came from, who our foremothers and forefathers were and how they handed this precious art down to us, generation by generation, for over one hundred and fifty years. Historic buildings remind us of a time when hand-making was honored and respected, from the clothes we wore to the buildings we worshiped in. The Paul Revere Foundry bell in the bell tower, cast in Boston's North End by the son of the famous Paul Revere, is an added attraction. Attendees get to ring it using the long rope in the hallway outside the sanctuary.

And, catered by For the Love of Food & Drink of Wells, Maine, the food is very, very good, which also gets talked about long after the event is over.

Fall Recipes

Home-Canned Applesauce

Here at the Parris House we do not have a very large apple orchard. In fact, we only have about four productive apple trees and, two of those provide most of our apples. The remaining few apple trees are up to one hundred and fifty years old, and put off a limited amount of fruit that we often do not even harvest. These are "witness trees," however, and they are valuable to us because of their history. It is very likely that these trees provided apples to the Parris family in the 19th century.

Prep Time: **1 hour**

Cook Time: **1-2 hours**

Canning Time: **20 minutes**

Yields: **1 gallon, 4 1-quart jars**

We find that our trees produce heavily every other year. In off years we sometimes have enough fruit for fresh pies, some apple-sauce, and other recipes, but when the trees are "on" we have so many apples that we must process and can or freeze them. After that we are often still using up the last of them a year later.

If you do not have apple trees, you're in luck! Picking apples at a local commercial orchard in the fall is a fun, inexpensive, and healthy way to spend a day. Commercial apple orchards are common in many areas and often offer additional attractions for their apple picking visitors. These can include hay-rides, live music, apple cider pressing, farm tours, and the sale of delicious apple products. Honestly, we never have quite that much fun harvesting our own trees, although we try to make a happy ritual of it just the same.

Canning applesauce is very easy and for that reason is a great introduction to boiling water bath canning if you have never done it before. Boiling water bath canning is the method used for fruits and vegetables that are acidic enough (about 4.0 pH or lower) to be preserved safely without fear of botulism developing in the food after canning. If the acidity of the food is too low, as is the case with most vegetables, meats, and broths, botulism spores, which survive boiling temperatures can still grow in it. They cannot grow in higher acid foods.

Because some foods can safely be preserved by boiling water bath canning and some require higher temperature pressure canning, unless you are an expert, I recommend that you get any of the great basic canning books available today and make them part of your cooking/homesteading library. You can also find information readily available online, your local university cooperative extension website being one of the very best resources. In fact, most university cooperative extensions even have a service for testing a sample of your canned batches to make sure that they are safe if you have any doubt at all. Batch testing is something many states require for licensed home canners intending to sell their wares, for good reason.

This recipe is for eighteen pounds of apples. I have found over the years that about eighteen pounds of our medium to medium-large apples yields about a gallon (four-quart jars) of applesauce. If you are canning commercially picked or purchased apples, go with about four pounds of apples per quart expected. You will want to use apples that are more firm/crisp than starchy/soft and more tart than sweet. McIntoshes are a common favorite. Breaburn, Fuji, and Golden Delicious are other good options. Experiment to see what you like best.

Ingredients

18 pounds freshly picked medium to medium-large apples
Optional: sugar and desired spices (I leave my applesauce plain so that I can use it in a variety of recipes later.)

You Will Need

Basic canning equipment and canning jars are readily available, especially during "canning season" from about the time the first fresh berries are available in late spring/early summer through the fall harvest season. You can find canning equipment at your local farm store, at many big box stores, at major supermarket chains, and online. The equipment is durable and reusable (except for the sealing lids) and therefore you will not have to buy it often if at all again.

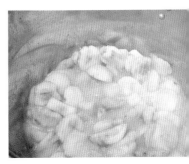

- 4 1-quart glass canning jars with screw top rings and never- before-used sealing lids, sterilized
- Large canning pot with rack on the inside bottom
- Canning funnel, sterilized
- Canning tongs, sterilized
- Magnetic lid handler
- Electric food processer or hand cranked food mill
- Large stock pot for cooking down the apples
- Large stock pot for sanitizing jars
- Small saucepan for sanitizing the screw top rings and sealing lids
- Hand peeler or crank style apple peeler
- Paring knife or apple slicer

Directions

1. Sterilize your jars. You may do this initially by running them through your dishwasher on the sanitize setting, but if you do not have a dishwasher, no worries. Even though I sanitize my jars and rings first in the dishwasher, I also keep a pot of simmering water on the stove in which to immerse the jars and lids to be extra sure that they are germ free prior to filling.

2. Peel and core your apples. Save those peels and cores for your chickens or the compost pile if either applies to your homestead.

3. Cut the apples in to small wedges either using a knife or an apple slicer. I cut each apple in to about ten or twelve wedges.

4. Put the wedges in to a large stock pot with just enough water to keep them from sticking to the bottom initially, not more than a quarter cup, and simmer them on low heat until they are cooked into a very soft state. This should take at least an hour and, when ready, the apples should be easily mashed with a fork or the back of a spoon.

It is during this cooking down process that you might choose to add sugar and spices to your taste. Just remember that if you want to be able to use the applesauce in baking or in other recipes, it is best to leave it plain. I prefer it plain just for eating also because I like to taste the subtle flavors of each year's apple harvest, but this is completely subjective.

5. During the last fifteen minutes or so of cooking the apples down, put your jars, funnel, and tongs in to the large pot of simmering water on your stove (not your canning pot) and put the rings in a smaller saucepan of simmering water. Do not put the sealing lids in there to simmer. You will sterilize them for a shorter time just before using them.

6. At this time also make sure the water in your boiling water canning pot is boiling! Leave the lid on until you are ready to put the jars in to avoid too much evaporation. You will need enough water in the canning pot to have about two inches of water over the submerged jars as they process. It is easier to ladle water out because you have too much in the pot than to add more and get it up to boiling again when you're ready to process.

7. With your tongs, remove the jars from the simmering bath, pouring as much water as possible out of them, and place them on a towel on your counter next to the food processor. Leave the rings in the smaller bath. The cooked apples will be extremely hot so please do these next steps with great care.

8. In batches, process the hot, cooked apples through your food processor or hand cranked food mill, and transfer it, using the sterilized canning funnel, into quart jars. Leave about one-half inch of headspace, or space between the top of the contents and the top of the jar.

NOTE: Why is it important to leave the right amount of headspace when canning? If you leave too little space, there is not enough room for the contents of the jar to expand during the boiling process and it could ooze out of the lid despite your best efforts, clearly not creating a good seal. If you leave too much space, too much air in the jar may prevent a strong vacuum seal and also leave enough air to oxidize the top of the contents.

9. Next, take your magnetic lid handler and dip the sealing lids, one at a time, into the sauce pan of simmering water. Hold them in the simmering water about fifteen seconds, shake off the excess water, and place them on top of the jars.

10. Use the magnetic lid handler to take the screw top rings out of the simmering water, place them over the lids, and screw them down finger tight. Do not overtighten.

11. Using your tongs, carefully lower your jars in to the canning bath, arranging them evenly on the bottom rack of the pot. You do not want them to fall over and be horizontal. They should be standing upright with approximately 2 inches of water above the submerged lids.

12. Put the lid on the canning pot to help ensure the boiling point is maintained and process (boil) the jars for twenty minutes.

NOTE: Processing times need to increase with altitude. This is because, due to changes in air pressure, the boiling point of water is lower after about 1000 feet in altitude and lowers additionally in subsequent increments. If you are above 1000 feet above sea level, please check your canning recipe for higher altitude processing times.

13. At the end of the processing time, remove the jars using your tongs and carefully place them on a towel on your counter to cool. Do not disturb them for about twenty-four hours! As they cool, listen for the tell-tale "plink" of the sealing lids. This is the final vacuum forming and sucking the lids down firmly as the jars cool. This is a sign that the jars are well sealed. You will know each jar is sealed if none of the lids "flex" when you touch them gently on their tops.

NOTE: What if a jar fails to seal? If a jar fails to seal, you have options. One, you could simply refrigerate it and treat yourself to the contents right away. Or, you could try reprocessing the jar with a new sealing lid. With applesauce,

reprocessing will likely not hurt the food. With other types of fruits and vegetables you may not want to reprocess because overcooking could negatively affect the texture and flavor of the food.

Pumpkin and/or Squash Soup with Late Fall Greens

Prep time: **15 minutes**

Cook time: **30-45 minutes**

Serves: **8**

Pumpkins and winter squashes make tasty and nutritious soups. We are often admonished to "eat all the colors" and soups made from these vegetables help us get our quota of yellow and orange while also providing a comfort food perfect for the crisper weather. This soup can be made all fall and winter long with the pumpkins and squashes you may have frozen from your own garden, but I have written the recipe with 15 ounce increments of pumpkin and squash in case you are using a standard sized store bought can of puree. The soup will be delicious either way.

Ingredients

1 tablespoon olive oil
3 cloves garlic, finely chopped
½ cup onion, finely chopped
15 ounces pumpkin puree
15 ounces winter squash puree
3 cups vegetable or chicken broth
1 tablespoon curry
1 teaspoon ginger
½ teaspoon white pepper
1 teaspoon salt or to taste
2 tablespoons brown sugar
1 cup whole milk or half and half
2 cups late summer/fall greens (kale, spinach, chard)
    chopped and sautéed in olive oil
Sour cream or plain Greek yogurt for garnish

Directions

1. Heat oil in the bottom of a stock pot
2. Add chopped garlic and onion and sauté until soft, but not brown
3. Add the pumpkin and squash puree and two cups of the broth, stirring continually so as not to allow it to burn on the bottom
4. Whisk in the rest of the broth and thoroughly combine
5. Add seasonings and brown sugar and allow to simmer for about 20-30 minutes, stirring often enough to prevent any browning or burning on the bottom

OPTIONAL: If you do not want the garlic and onions to be chunky in the soup, turn off the heat and use a stick blender at this point to blend the soup perfectly smooth

6. Turn off heat and add the milk or half and half and whisk in until thoroughly mixed.
7. Ladle into shallow bowls and garnish with a teaspoon of sour cream or plain Greek yogurt if desired
8. Add a sprinkling of the sautéed greens either directly into the serving bowl of soup or as a side accompaniment. I do not recommend adding it to the main pot of soup, rather, allow each person to use the greens as they wish. My preference? I like the greens on the side as a counterpoint to the sweet spiciness of the soup.

Honey Ginger Apple Pie
with Honeyed Top Crust

Ingredients

6-8 medium to large fresh apples, not too sweet or starchy
    (Macs are readily available and good for baking)
1 double pie crust, homemade or store bought
1/3 cup honey plus enough to brush on the top crust
¼ cup all-purpose flour
3 pats butter
¾ teaspoon ginger
Pinch salt
Dash cinnamon

Prep time: **30 minutes**

Bake time: **40 minutes**

A NOTE ON PIE CRUSTS: I do not make my own pie crusts. I know. I've learned a lot about DIY since moving to Maine almost two decades ago, but this one still eludes perfection or anything near it plus I'm often just so pressed for time. I buy good quality pie crusts locally and use them in my pie baking. If you have a wonderful family recipe for homemade pie crust, that will make this recipe all the more delicious.

Directions

1. Preheat oven to 325 degrees Fahrenheit.
2. Wash, peel, and core your apples and then slice them into wide pieces, about ½ inch thick. This is a very rustic pie.
3. Put the apple slices into a large bowl and toss with the flour, ginger, salt, and cinnamon.
4. Add 1/3 cup honey to the mix and coat the apples thoroughly. The dry ingredients will blend in with the honey. Taste an apple piece at this point and adjust to your liking. For example, you may prefer more ginger.

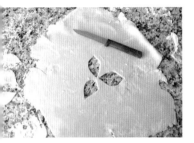

5. Line a deep-dish pie plate with the bottom crust.

6. Turn the apple mixture into the bottom crust and place the three pats of butter evenly spaced on top of the apples.

7. Roll out or unroll your top crust and place it on a floured surface. You can use a paring knife to freehand carve some leaves or shapes out of the top crust to vent it, or you can use a decorative cookie cutter or crust cutting tool.

8. Place the top crust over the top of the pie, decorating as you wish with the cut-out pieces. I always keep mine very simple and rustic, but if you like the pie decorating process get as elaborate as you like.

9. Brush the top crust lightly with honey. It is not necessary to hit every single area of the crust but do coat most of it.

10. Bake on the center oven rack for forty minutes and check for browning on the top crust. If you do not have enough browning, pop it back in, possibly a little higher up in the oven, but look at it frequently, at least every five minutes, until it is browned to your liking.

11. When browned to your liking, remove the pie from the oven and cool on a wire rack. You might have a little honey pooling in the nooks and crannies. Feel free to gently rotate the pie a little bit to allow that honey to go down into the pie vents or you could brush it over the top of the pie some more. Either method results in deliciousness.

OPTIONAL: serve with the homemade French vanilla ice cream from our Spring recipes section, perhaps with some honey added, or whip up some whipped cream with a little ginger added in or sprinkled on top. If you are quite serious about your ginger, serve with crystallized ginger candy.

A NOTE ABOUT THE HONEY WE USE: Of course, we have our own honey from the Parris House apiary, but we don't use our "first quality" honey for baking. When we extract our honeycomb, we bottle and sell the honey that comes out of the comb via the extractor and which we then filter and call our "first quality" honey. However, that's not all the honey we get or use for our own purposes. My husband will later strain honey out of the wax cappings bucket and filter it as well. This yields a surprising amount of honey and we use it at home for tea, baking, cooking, or just spreading on toast. If you do not have your own honey, I would encourage you to experiment with a variety of honeys available from local beekeepers because each flavor profile will slightly change the taste and aroma of this pie.

WINTER

Far from Dormant

Winter at the Parris House brings challenges. Paris Hill village is situated atop a hill and the Parris House is at the north end with an unobstructed lookout to the northwest. This affords a spectacular mountain view but in winter it also leaves the house, porch, and barn vulnerable to the strong northwesterly winds that carry in most of our weather systems. The winter beatings have been severe enough to rip centuries-old shutters from the house, encrust windows in ice, and blow so much snow in to the driveway that a front-end loader has at times been necessary to remove it. It also creates special concerns for our bees and chickens, although as you might suspect, they have their own natural defenses. Paris, Maine receives several feet of snow a year. Because of climate change this may well be different in the coming years, bringing new challenges for those of us who, regardless of the hardships, love our North Atlantic seasons.

A Western Maine winter is not for everyone, though, not even for some Mainers. We have the "snowbird" phenomenon, which means that some of our population goes south for the winter every year. Some go to the Carolinas or to Florida, some just go anywhere it might be warmer. I personally think they're missing out, and when I voice this, they say the usual things: "Yes, we're missing freezing to death," "Yes, we're missing four figure heating bills," "Yes, we're missing a visit to the hospital from an icy trip and fall." But there are good things to miss too.

The crystalline wonderland of winter in Maine makes for my second favorite season here. For every hardship she inflicts in winter, Mother Nature supplies a blessing. We are within an easy drive of three major Maine ski areas: Shawnee Peak, Sunday River, and Sugarloaf, and quite a few smaller ski mountains. We have an incredible local network of cross-country skiing and snowshoe trails and for some Mainers the frozen lakes mean ice fishing and, if the snow is cleared, skating and hockey. Recently we've been seeing fat-tire bikes on the roads in winter and, of course, many people enjoy the snowmobile trail network as well. The best way to approach winter in Maine is to get outside where the sheer spectacle of its frozen beauty is a highly effective distraction from its discomforts.

Having said all that, winter also provides the indoor time we need to catch up on things our warmer weather activities prevent the rest of the year. The days are very short in Maine this time of year, with darkness coming well before five p.m. for much of it, so it's best to know what you'll do with your indoor hours as well. For this reason, it is the perfect time to do crafting, try new recipes, and enjoy the harvest you preserved in the summer and fall.

Often in winter, I think about how hard this season must have been for generations past. Without central heating, residents of Paris Hill in the early nineteenth century would have resorted to heating with the many fireplaces in their homes. Later, parlor stoves would come into common use, providing more convenient and efficient heating. Yet, it is doubtful that rooms were the relatively toasty 65 degrees or more that many people are used to today.

While we obviously have central heating at the Parris House today, we also have a big wood burning stove in the kitchen that heats a large portion of the first floor and makes a wonderful stove for cast iron cooking, as you will see in the winter recipe section. We also have one of the best defenses an antique home has against winter drafts: doors everywhere. As they likely did two centuries ago, we use the doors on each interior room and even on the hallways to manage the flow of heat in the house during the winter. When I was a real estate broker, I would talk to my old house clients about just how well this works. Many new homes are designed as "open concept," which may be fine with today's modern heating systems, but the old-time smaller rooms divided from one another by doors afforded our ancestors, and us, efficient options too.

More amazing to me than the cold that must have been endured indoors is how roads were kept passable after significant snowstorms. Huge and heavy rollers, drawn by teams of horses, were sometimes used to pack down snow in the streets giving a firmer foundation for sleighs. Old fashioned hand shoveling, which we still do today to keep entryways and walkways clear, would have been the norm as well. It's a common sight in Maine to see front entrances on homes abandoned to the snow in winter, with only side or back entrances kept shoveled and accessible. This is a luxury unavailable to us at the Parris House because the rug hooking studio here is open year-round and our patrons come in the front door. For this reason, we refer to the ever-increasing walls of snow on either side of the front walkway as "the hooker chute." I have shoveled the chute on days when the sides of it were as tall as I am. Often I get too warm in the process, take my coat off, and toss it atop one side.

The bottom line is, winter is genuinely hard work in Maine and there is no getting around it. Big snowstorms, resulting in "snow days" can sometimes seem a welcome excuse to take it a bit easier, if only for that day.

SABBATHDAY LAKE SHAKERS' HOLIDAY FAIR

One of our favorite events in early December is the Sabbathday Lake Shaker's Holiday Fair. Founded in 1783, the Sabbathday Lake Shaker Village in New Gloucester, Maine, is not like the other Shaker sites in the United States. The Sabbathday Lake location is a living community. As of this writing, the community is home to three living Shakers who lead the religious services and with the assistance of their able staff and volunteers, continue to run the farm and "fancy goods" businesses. In addition to the farming and retail operations, the Shakers host a steady stream of visitors each year during their spring, summer, and fall open hours and event days. They host scores of art, craft, and making workshops with teachers from all over the area. I teach rug hooking there and my husband, Bill, teaches cold process soap making. There are two Shaker stores on the premises that sell artisanal products and décor, food products, herbs, teas, books, household items, soap, yarns spun from the wool of the Shakers' sheep, and more. Annual events include Open Farm Day in July, Harvest Festival in October, and the Holiday Fair in December.

On the day of the Holiday Fair it's best to get there early! At times it's standing-room-only in the Shaker store with visitors pouring out to the sidewalk where gorgeous hand-crafted wreaths are sold. The goodies inside that generate intense interest and often sell out quickly are Brother Arnold's pickles (hot or dill), the delicious cheeses, and the Shaker fruitcakes. Yes, these fruitcakes are the good kind.

While the Sabbathday Lake Shaker Village is remarkable as a historic landmark and working farm, it is also an oasis of peace for visitors. Because at its heart and in its purpose this place is a spiritual community, there is a serenity to it, even on the busiest days, that is deeply felt but hard to articulate. Even in this, the Shakers are generous, offering retreats for men and for women during the year and keeping their worship services open to the public.

Winter Homesteading

Cleaning Hooked and Other Rugs with Snow

Here in New England, we have no shortage of snow in winter. Even during unseasonably warm winters, there will always be some snowstorms that provide just the right kind of snow for the age-old technique of cleaning rugs outdoors. I admit that when I first moved to Maine and heard of this method of cleaning rugs, I was skeptical. It turns out that our resourceful ancestors were on to something. If you live in a snowy area, give this method a try with your area rugs this winter and enjoy the fresh air, mild exercise, and results it yields.

This method is particularly good for rugs that you do not want to, or because of size, materials, or construction, cannot put into a washing machine or have commercially cleaned. This applies to most hand hooked rugs and many vintage or antique rugs. As a caveat, be sure that your rugs are in solid condition before employing snow cleaning. If your rug is fragile or deteriorating in any way, this is not a good method for cleaning. Also, if you have reason to suspect your rug is not colorfast, this method is also best avoided, although so are many other methods in that case.

You will need:

- The rug or rugs you'd like to clean. Make sure you have enough space to hang them to dry when finished. If not, just do them one at a time or in batches according to the drying space you have.
- Your winter outerwear. You're doing this outside!

- A clean broom with soft enough bristles that it will not harm or inadvertently pull on the loops of your hand hooked or other rugs. I use a broom with firm but not large or stiff nylon bristles. As much as I love traditional corn brooms that were probably used for this purpose in generations past, I think the modern nylon brooms are a little gentler for our rugs.
- A few inches of fresh, fine, powdery snow. There's some leeway here on the texture of the snow, but what you do not want is snow that is heavy or too wet. If the temperatures are above freezing and the snow is melting, pick a colder, dryer day to clean your rugs. Additionally, use a patch of snow that's very fresh and clean. You don't want to defeat the purpose by adding dirt, salt, or sand to your rug!

Instructions

1. Lay your rug face down in the snow. Leave it there for ten to thirty minutes or so until it stiffens a bit in the cold.
2. Take your broom and beat the rug all over with it on the reverse side. You do not need to be overly gentle with this because you are loosening all the stray dirt and allowing it to fall out in to the snow beneath.
3. Lift the rug up and examine the snow underneath. You should see bits of dirt, pet hair, and other debris that has come out of the rug. If the rug was very dirty, you may even see an overall darkening of the snow beneath it. If you think there's more dirt left in the rug, pop it back down and beat it with the broom again.

4. Next, take the rug and lay it down, face side up, in another clean patch of snow.

5. Sweep a thin layer of snow on to the surface of the rug. Yes, this feels counterintuitive, but just do it!

6. Allow snow to sit on the rug's surface for a few minutes and then vigorously start sweeping the snow off the surface of the rug. This is when the magic becomes apparent. You should see a brighter, cleaner surface than when you started. You may repeat the process if you think there is still some additional cleaning to do or if you notice a particular area that's not quite as clean as the others.

7. Pick up the rug and shake or brush all of the excess snow off of the rug.

8. Hang the rug to dry in a clean, well ventilated area. The rug should not be too wet after this process if the snow was relatively dry and powdery and the temperatures outside were low.

Overwintering Bees

Of all of the homesteading activities we've conducted at the Parris House, overwintering bees has been the most challenging and tenuous. Our first season, we lost two out of two hives over the winter. The second season, we had three hives going in to winter and again, lost them all. Finally, the third season, we had four hives survive a brutally cold and snowy Maine winter with a 100% survival rate! Imagine our joy after our first two seasons of disappointment.

There are so many factors involved in whether or not your bees survive the winter that I can not possibly cover them all here. However, I will cover a few of the major causes of hive death during winter and suggest to you that you do the unpleasant task of "hive autopsy" in the spring should your colonies not survive. Hive autopsy is the process of taking apart your dead hive, looking at it frame by frame, and trying to determine why your colony died.

Four major causes of colony death in winter are viruses vectored by the dreaded varroa mite, excessive moisture in the hive, vermin entering the hive, and starvation. There are measures that can be taken to try to prevent all of these causes.

Varroa Vectored Viruses

It is very important that you keep an eye on your colonies for varroa infestation during the active beekeeping seasons of spring, summer, and early fall. Varroa mites are implicated in what is popularly referred to as "colony collapse disorder," although this is a complex phenomenon and it is not completely clear what causes it. In the case of our first two seasons' overwintering failures, we believe that viruses vectored by an excessive mite load going in to winter were what killed our colonies. After both unsuccessful seasons, we "autopsied" our hives. By this I mean we went through each hive looking for evidence of what had killed our bees. We found that many of our dead bees had deformed wings and shortened abdomens, telltale signs of viruses that can prove fatal to a colony.

Testing via sugar or alcohol rolling of a sample of bees, and, if necessary, treating your hives for varroa infestation in late summer and fall can go a long way toward avoiding this fate. In our first successful season with a 100% overwinter survival rate, we had taken special care to make sure the hives had a very low mite load going in to winter.

Please note that getting the mite load to zero is not a realistic goal. If you have bee hives in Maine, or anywhere in the United States, you are going to have varroa mites. It is simply a matter of managing that load with testing and treatment to the best of your ability.

Excessive Moisture in the Hive

If your hives are not adequately ventilated and controlled for condensation, too much moisture can build up in the hive creating conditions in which your cluster of bees simply can not maintain a survivable temperature.

Bees avoid freezing to death in winter by clustering in a tight ball within the hive. If the hive is relatively dry inside, temperature can be maintained by the cluster, however, if condensation is present or, worse, dripping on to the cluster, keeping warm will be increasingly difficult for the bees.

We use a Homasote board on top of the inner cover to help absorb moisture. We also make sure that the upper and lower entrances to the hives are clear of ice or snow, allowing air to flow through. This may feel counterintuitive, especially on the briskest winter days, but it is not excessive outdoor temperatures that often kill bees. It is condensation in the hive.

To enhance ventilation further, some beekeepers use very thin shims between the inner and outer cover to create even more air flow through the hive. We have not done this, finding that condensation seems well controlled without that measure.

Vermin in the Hive

While you want good air flow through your hives in winter, you do not want any openings large enough to allow mice or voles to enter! This was another rookie mistake we made our first year and upon opening one of our hives discovered that much of the comb had been chewed through and nested in by voles. This added more work to the process of cleaning and preparing the hives for a new season and contributed to the distress and ultimate death of that colony.

The solution to this is relatively easy. Get good lower entrance guards for your hives and put them on late in the season prior to winter. We use metal entrance guards with small holes that allow bees in and out and provide good ventilation but prevent vermin from entering the hives. Alternatively, you can staple a metal grid "cloth" over the lower entrance, choosing one with holes small enough to prevent invasion but large enough for the bees to enter and exit. This basically looks like chicken wire only with smaller openings and is available in a variety of sizes at your local hardware store.

Starvation

This is one of the saddest causes of colony death. When a hive has starved you will often find the bee bodies left in the hive, headfirst in the comb cells with their tails sticking out. Interestingly, colonies do not starve one bee at a time. They starve almost simultaneously and are usually not scattered around the frames when you find them dead.

While sometimes starvation occurs because the cluster is too small and weak to move to nearby food stores, bees can also starve over winter by simply running out of food. This is why we always leave plenty of honey on the hives going into winter. Our hives are composed of 8-frame medium boxes and going in to winter we leave at least two full boxes of honey on the hives for them to feed on. Were we running 10-frame deeps we would leave at least one full box of honey on each hive. Additionally, we add hard sugar candy to each hive as extra insurance in case our bees eat all of their honey during the winter and still need more food.

Bees will generally cluster in the lower boxes toward the beginning of winter and work their way up toward the upper

boxes as they feed on the stored honey to survive. Placing the hard sugar candy on top of the frames in the top box puts the food right where they'll need it when they've eaten through the top box of honey.

Making sugar candy for bees is easy and, I'd argue, kind of fun. You can make "candy boards" by getting an extra inner hive cover and spreading the sugar candy in to it, then placing it sugar-side-down above the top frames on the top box, but we found it easier to just make the candy in disposable pie plates and then place it directly on the top frames over a bit of newspaper.

Here's how you make the candy, install it in the hives, and continue to check it throughout late winter and early spring to make sure your bees are eating like kings, or more aptly, like queens.

Sugar Candy for Bees

For each tin of sugar candy, you will need:

- 5 pounds sugar
- 1 pint water
- Disposable aluminum pie tin
- Candy thermometer or infrared thermometer

Dissolve the sugar into the water in a heavy pot on the stove, stirring continually to keep it from burning on the bottom. Bring it to a boil, uncovered, still stirring, until the mixture reaches 234 degrees Fahrenheit. It will start to feel pretty thick.

Pour the candy in to the pie tin and allow to cool completely. It's usually cold enough when we are making these to just put them out on our porch and allow them to harden up quickly.

Installing the Candy in the Hives

This should be done very quickly if the weather is cold (below 45 degrees Fahrenheit or so) when you are opening the hives so as not to chill the bees any more than is absolutely necessary. It should truly take less than a minute. To save on open time, pop the sugar patties out of the pie tins before opening the hives.

Remove the outer and inner cover, place a shim as shown to accommodate the height of the sugar patty on to the top frames, place the sugar patty on to that, and close up the hive. That's it! If you happen to have bees already on the top frames, very gently brush them out of the area you intend to place the sugar on, taking care to disturb them as little as humanly possible.

Checking Back

We check the sugar supply on our hives weekly or as the weather allows once we see that the bees are well in to eating it. This may seem excessive, but at this point it is usually very late in the winter and we want to make sure there is no way for them to starve after surviving the worst of the season.

NOTE: Why hard candy and not syrup feed like we use in the spring? It may seem that the answer to this is because the syrup would freeze, but the more important answer is that providing liquid syrup to bees this time of year would introduce moisture, and therefore condensate, in to the hive which is what we do not want in cold weather.

I cannot emphasize enough that bee colonies are complex living things. They are by far the most complex "livestock" we have ever cared for and overwintering is perhaps the most challenging aspect of beekeeping. For this reason, I strongly recommend that you have a mentor, take classes offered through your state university cooperative extension, adult education programs, or local beekeepers, and join your local bee club for support. Additionally, read, read, read! You will find that if you ask five beekeepers a question you may get ten different answers, and what works for one beekeeper may not be a preferred method for another. Beekeeping is both art and science and there is no substitute for experience. The seasonal beekeeping sections offered here are a general reference and overview and you will find that the learning never ends as you care for these amazing and beautiful creatures.

Tips on Wintering Chickens

Many people worry about how their chickens will fare in winter, and I did too. I soon learned that chickens are resilient and will do very well in winter with common sense precautions. However, some things that may seem to be common sensical are not or are even downright dangerous. Here are some dos and don'ts for keeping your chickens happy and healthy over the winter.

Keep winter hardy chicken breeds.

When we order our chicks in the spring, we pay attention to which breeds are listed as cold hardy. In our case we keep Golden Comets, Buff Orpingtons, Ameraucanas, Black Austrolorpes, Araucanas, and Laced Wyandotte. This combination also gives us a lovely variety of light brown, deep brown, and blue-green eggs.

Do *Not* Heat the Coop

One of the saddest things that can happen to families with backyard chickens is a coop fire. Not only is this obviously a death sentence to the flock, but it also endangers the lives and property of the family. Each winter in Maine we hear of fires originating in a chicken coop and many of these are the result of well-meaning chicken keepers attempting to heat the coop. This is simply unnecessary. Your hens will huddle for warmth and if otherwise well fed and healthy this is perfectly sufficient for them.

Check to Make Sure the Coop is Secure from Predators

This is a great time to make sure your coop is secure. Here in

Maine our centuries old barn does not sit perfectly still, especially in winter. As the ground shifts and heaves, so too does our barn shift and heave. Our coop is a normally very secure room at the back end of the barn with a fenced and covered run for the hens out behind it. However, it is still possible for very small shifts to create equally small, but dangerous, openings to our coop floor or walls. Predators don't need a very big hole for access, especially in winter when they may be hungrier than usual. It's a good idea to examine your coop regularly for security, cover any potential breaches with wood or chicken wire, and just scan the coop each time you're in it for any changes.

Occasionally Feed Them Warm Oatmeal as a Treat

In extremely cold weather it's a nice treat for your hens to have some warm oatmeal, perhaps with some treats mixed

in. They love it and who can resist the charm of hens eagerly clamoring for this welcome bit of tasty warmth? Oatmeal contains nutrients that are beneficial to chickens and makes a great vehicle for treats as a mix-in. Some treats that you can mix into the oatmeal are berries, mealworms, chicken-friendly seeds, herbs, or even your vegetable scraps.

Relatively recently there was a controversy in cyberspace about feeding chickens oatmeal. I have read all sides of this issue and am going with the preponderance of evidence and the most reliable sources which all indicate that giving your chickens warm oatmeal on the coldest days as a treat is not only acceptable, it's beneficial. I view the controversy as an important reminder that there are many ways to approach most homesteading skills and it is best to be wary about any source that is either militant about one single way or seems to have an agenda of any kind.

Of course, oatmeal is nutritious for us too and since it's extremely economical to buy and prepare, just make extra for the hens. When you have returned from the coop, perhaps cold and with snow on your clothes, you'll be grateful for your oatmeal too.

Consider a Heated Waterer in Extremely Cold Weather

Be judicious about this because whenever you introduce an electric appliance to your coop you are adding an element of risk, even if slight. While heating the coop itself is unnecessary and not worth any risk at all, heating the water can be necessary under specific circumstances. If you are not finding the water frozen on a regular basis, especially if you are able to take warm water out to the coop or run area often, then a heated waterer is not necessary. However, if you have a persistent problem with frozen water, especially if you are away for extended hours every day, you might consider a heated waterer.

There are a variety of heated waterers or deicers on the market. There are heated platforms atop which you can put your standard metal waterer and there are plug-in plastic waterers that are a single unit, but still the gravity fed type like the metal waterer. There are nipple-style heated feeders and also just large open heated bowls.

We like either the plug-in plastic waterers or the simplest solution, the heated platform on which you can put a standard waterer. We do not prefer open bowls of water for our hens, particularly in winter, because they tend to splash the water around. Once this water is splashed around it can refreeze on other surfaces or get the chickens themselves a little wet, which we are trying to avoid.

You may recall that in a previous season we recommended you check over all the electrical wiring in your coop to make sure that it is safe and in good condition. If you feel this is beyond your expertise, have an electrician do it for you. While a heated waterer does not get hot enough by itself to likely cause a fire in your coop, bad wiring switched on to power it can. Therefore, always keep your coop wiring meticulously maintained and regularly inspected.

Do *Not* Get Too Concerned about Mucking the Coop as Regularly as You Would in Warm Weather.

I understand the desire to keep the coop clean. This is an important part of keeping your flock healthy, however, in wintertime it may not be possible to muck the coop as often as you would in warm weather. It is fine to use what many people call a "deep litter" technique in winter with your hens, especially if you have done a good job of keeping the coop dry, undampened by any exterior leaks or cracks where snow can come in and melt or by a waterer that is not properly sealed.

Toward the end of fall, right before the snow flies, give the coop a thorough cleaning. You can refer back to the big spring coop cleaning section earlier in the book. Really get it cleaned out and ready for a winter of either no mucking or infrequent mucking.

When the coop is clean and dry, put down a layer of pine shavings, straw, or a mix of both. We strongly prefer pine shavings during the other three seasons, but straw can be a nice addition going in to winter. You are going to be building on this initial layer as the season goes on.

When you see that the litter isn't looking fresh, add more and turn it like you would compost. Keep doing this throughout the season and encourage the hens to also turn it by scratching at it. Throwing some food or treats on to the floor of the coop encourages them to do this.

This method should keep the coop smelling fresh and the hens healthy throughout the winter.

Make Sure the Coop is Sized Appropriately for the Flock

If your coop is cavernous in proportion to the size of your flock, it may be a little harder for them to keep warm. Remember that the rule of thumb is two to four square feet per hen. Having a generously sized coop in other seasons is great, but if your coop is huge compared to your flock, you may want to consider partitioning it for the season creating a cozier space for them.

Continue Feeding Them Vegetable Scraps and Treats.

It's less convenient this time of year to take your vegetable scraps out to the hen house but do it anyway. The variety helps with the hens' nutrition and helps to keep them active as they peck through it. Additionally, all of the extra vegetation culled from the garden is a thing of the past in winter, so any nice scraps that come from the household meal preparation are a plus. This is also a good time to keep chicken treats, like bags of dried mealworms, in the pantry so you can add a little to each batch of scraps you take out to your birds.

Do *Not* Use Artificial Light to Keep Them Laying.

Hens have a natural laying cycle. As the days get shorter and colder here in the north, they naturally stop laying as many eggs and may even stop laying altogether for a time. Light stimulates a hen's pineal gland, which sends the hormonal signal to lay eggs. Hens need at least fourteen to sixteen hours of daylight per day to keep laying regularly and in Maine during the winter, we're not getting anywhere near that much daylight.

We do not interfere with this natural laying cycle because we want to avoid stressing our hens. We believe it is healthier to allow them their natural rest season. Throughout the year we have times when we are selling many dozens of eggs to our neighbors and customers because of the abundance our flock provides, knowing that there will be other times when we barely have enough for our own family. This is the price of happy, healthy hens and the most delicious and nutrient filled eggs we could hope for.

If you are relying on egg sales as an indispensable source of income, you might consider artificial lighting but only to the threshold levels that provide the fourteen to sixteen total hours of light, not twenty-four hours a day. Lighting the coop all night will interfere with the hens' ability to sleep, which again, creates a stressful and unhealthy situation. Coop lighting that's on for extended periods can also be one more fire hazard if not very carefully installed and monitored.

Most of us are not raising and keeping chickens as a make or break income source and therefore most flocks should be allowed to respond naturally to the seasons without artificial lighting in the coop.

Allow Them to Go Outside.

Contrary to how it may seem at times, your hens know how to protect themselves from many threats. One of these is freezing to death. Give your hens the opportunity to get outside every day, even in winter, in their protected run area. Some may decide to venture out and some may not but open the coop door and let them have the choice. They will not go outside if they are uncomfortable doing so.

It can be nice to lay a blanket of straw on top of the snow so that if they venture out, they have something to walk on and grab on to. If you are concerned about their wattles and combs getting frost bitten, which is possible, put a little petroleum jelly on them. We have never had a frostbitten chicken, but it is something to look out for. In our case I think it has helped that we choose cold hardy breeds with smaller wattles and combs to begin with.

I don't recommend free ranging your hens in winter, though, at least not completely unattended. Predators are hungry this time of year and chickens are the perfect fast food for them.

If you follow these practices and precautions, you will find that your chickens are comfortable and healthy all winter long and will be ready to resume their more abundant laying habits when the days start lengthening in the spring.

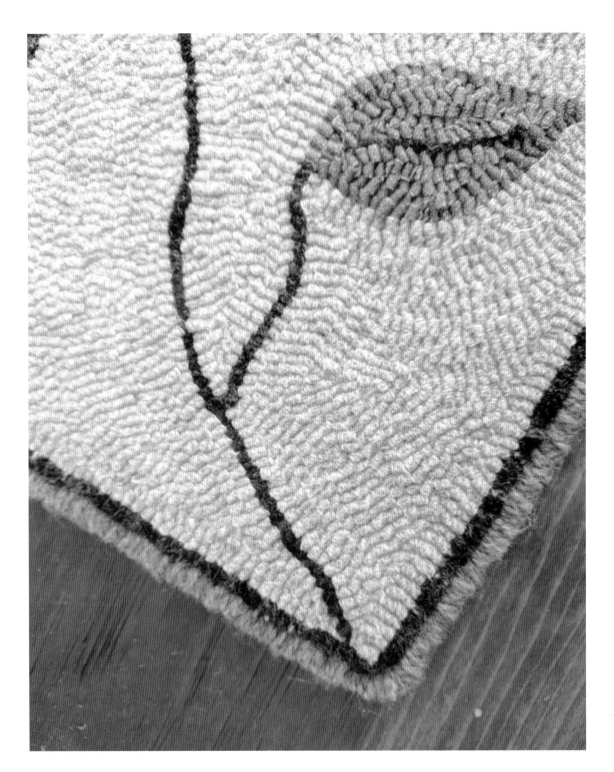

Heritage Skills for Contemporary Living

Winter Projects

Hit or Miss Rug Hooking— A Heritage Design

Winter is a great time to take on larger crafting projects, the kind we think we may not have time for during the warmer months. It's also a great time to organize your home and particularly, your crafting area and supplies. Hit or Miss style rug hooking is a great way to approach these goals.

Hit or Miss rugs are foundational to the heritage of North American rug hooking. They are possibly one of the earliest types of rugs made in New England and the Canadian Maritimes and are found in every generation of rug hooking, from the 1800s through today. Because North American rug hooking began as a practical craft using materials already found in the household, Hit or Miss style evolved organically. So, what is it?

Hit or Miss rugs are made using whatever materials you have on hand in a relatively random way but organized within a general pattern, often a geometric. One of the most common designs in Hit or Miss rug hooking is a simple block motif. The traditional hit or miss rug design is made up of a grid of blocks, all the same size and often in convenient proportions (e.g. each 6" x 6"), with a border around the grid. The blocks are then hooked in neat rows using whatever wool or fabric is at hand, with little or no planning for the colors used from strip to strip. One block is hooked in horizontal lines, the next in vertical lines, the next in horizontal, and so on. This creates a timeless abstract result that

is at home both in an antique farmhouse and a contemporary apartment.

Because the Hit or Miss rug does not require a consistent or uniform palette of materials, it also makes for a great group or community project. At the Parris House, our Tuesday rug hooking group created a 3' x 5' Hit or Miss style rug to be raffled for the benefit the Maine Medical Center's Kidney Transplant Family Assistance Program. One member of the group would take the rug home each week to work on some squares or the border and even though we had as many as a dozen artisans with different wool stashes and styles work on the rug, the result was perfect.

This project is a partial hit or miss with some Maine botanical motifs mixed in every other block. I think this adds an authentic Maine character to the rug while still in keeping with the hit or miss tradition. This is a sizeable mat, large enough to warm your toes on by the side of the bed or near a favorite chair, but small enough to be manageable for someone new to the craft. If you would like this rug to be larger, you can simply repeat the pattern, proportionally, on a larger piece of linen.

So, here's your chance to go through your wool pieces, yarns, old tee shirts, what have you, cut them in to strips and make a brand-new rug for your home while cleaning up excess materials.

You Will Need

- Rug hooking primitive linen (or rug warp or monks' cloth), at least 24" x 32" but 1 yard (approximately 36" x 64") will give you extra to use on another project
- Wool or other fabric strips, cut to no more than about a ¼" in width but a variety of sizes is fine
- Large quilting hoop or a rug hooking frame
- Rug hook made for primitive size cuts

- Wool cutter or rotary cutter
- Yarn for whipstitch finishing
- Large finishing needle, as is used in knitting

Pattern Instructions

1. Leaving a 4" allowance around your design, draw a rectangle on your linen that is 16" x 24," being very careful to make sure all straight lines are on the grain of the linen. This will be the size of your rug. Your entire piece of linen, once the pattern is laid out within it with 4" to spare all around, should measure 24" x 32."

2. Within our 16" x 24" rectangle, draw a grid of 6 - 8" x 8" blocks, again making sure that your straight lines are on the grain of the linen. You will have two blocks in the width direction and three blocks in the length direction, with 6 blocks total.

3. Now, divide three of your blocks, alternating between them, in to four – 4" x 4" blocks. These will be your hit or miss blocks.

4. In the remaining three whole 8" x 8" blocks, draw your Maine botanical motifs: pine tassel, birch leaf, and fiddlehead.

5. Zig zag, serge, or duct tape the edges of your linen to keep it from raveling.

Hooking Tips

Refer to the basic hooking instructions in the Spring section of this book.

- Hook along each line of the overall grid, creating defined edges for the outside lines and the blocks, both the 8" x 8" blocks and the smaller 4" x 4" blocks. You may use black or some other color for this, but for this step use a single color. You are

outlining the blocks on this step.

- Hook each hit or miss block in straight lines, pulling a random worm of wool or fabric from your collection of cut pieces or, you could color coordinate them if you like. For adjacent blocks, hook one block horizontally, then hook the one next to it vertically, alternating so that each block is next to one hooked in the perpendicular direction.

- Hook each botanical block by first hooking the plant element, hooking a line or two around the interior of the square perimeter, and then echoing out the background from around the plant element.

- If desired, hook some rows, as many as desired, around the entire perimeter of the finished grid as a border. You may hook this in the same color you used to hook the grid outlines or choose something else.

Whipstitch Finishing

This is the easiest way to finish a hooked rug and creates a very traditional look.

1. Steam and block your finished rug. Refer to the spring hooking project for steaming and blocking instructions.

2. Remove the excess linen around the edges. It is very important to do this in a way that will prevent the linen from raveling. You may either use a serging/overlock machine to stitch around your rug, leaving about ¼ to ½ inch of linen, or you may use a conventional sewing machine, zigzag stitching two to three times leaving the same amount of linen around the rug and then hand cut the excess off.

3. Find some nice wool or other high-quality yarn and a knitting finishing or tapestry needle. Thread about a 2-foot length through your finishing needle.

4. Starting somewhere along a side of the rug, not at the corner, roll the linen edge of the rug back on itself and bring the threaded needle up through the linen as close as possible to the edge of the loops, leaving a short tail on the underside that will be caught and held down by the subsequent stitches.

5. Start a whipstitch by wrapping the yarn around the edge of the linen with each stitch, coming through as close as possible to the loop edges and lining the stitches up one next to the other to completely cover the linen. The object is to have no linen showing.

6. When you approach the corners, it may be necessary to overlap some of the stitches to completely cover the corners as you work your way around.

7. Continue all the way around, rethreading the needle with new yarn as needed and securing the ends underneath of the whip stitching.

Winter Wool, Linen Stars, and Pine Trees Garland

Fiber art garlands are a wonderful way to bring cheerful accents into your home during the winter months when we don't have fresh flowers from our gardens or blossoms from our trees. Much like the hit or miss hooked rugs, fiber art garlands are a great way to use up scraps and stash from other projects. This is an imaginative opportunity for you to get very creative and make your garland in any style that suits your tastes and environment, from simple modern to country primitive to high Victorian. There are no rules and there is no right or wrong way. The garland I'm going to show you is a simple snowflakes and stars motif, modern with a nod to the primitive, but tailor these basic guidelines to your life and home.

These pennants are a pretty bold size, drawn on standard 8.5" x 11" paper resulting in their being 11" long. I like the garland at this scale for some of the places I hang it at the Parris House, but as with any project, you can scale the size up or down to your liking.

You Will Need

1/8-yard burlap or rug hooking linen (This is a great way to use up burlap or linen scraps left over from hooking projects.)
1/8-yard silver/gray wool, washed and dried
1 yard white/cream wool, washed and dried
1 skein silver gray worsted weight yarn
2 skeins silver/gray embroidery floss or 1 ball of perle cotton

Embroidery needle

Straight pins

Natural or cotton cording or silver ribbon, about 8 feet

Tapestry needle

Sewing scissors/shears

Pennant, pine tree, and star templates

Fabric bonding material (optional)

White glue or fray check

Waxed paper

Disposable fine paint brush

Instructions

1. Cut out the pine tree, star, and pennant templates so that you have shapes for cutting out your fabric pieces.

2. For all of the following cut-outs, you might layer the wool or burlap so that you can cut out all of the shapes at one time.

3. Pin the pine tree and star templates on to the silver/gray wool and cut out three of each.

4. Pin the pine tree and star templates on to the linen or burlap and cut out three of each. Beekeepers, if you have any tiny linen or burlap scraps left, save them to burn in your bee smoker.

5. Pin the pennant shape on the white/cream wool and cut out six. You will notice that the pennant shape is two triangular sides to be folded over to make a single pennant. You can either cut them out on the fold of the fabric or figure out whatever the most efficient use of the fabric is.

6. Pin together each folded pennant an inch below the fold line. This will serve as the mark under which you center the fabric pine tree or star for each side and also be the marker for the sleeve through which your cording will go.

7. Pin your pine trees and stars on the pennants to experiment with the way you'd like them. You can choose to have a burlap pine tree on one side of the pennant with a wool pine tree on the other, or otherwise mix and match the shapes side to side however you like. Aesthetically, I like it best when the burlap and wool are alternating once the entire garland is assembled. This experimentation is best done prior to adhering the shapes to the pennants as follows.

8. For the wool pine trees and stars: center the shape and, using the instructions for the fabric bonding material, bond the shape in to place. Alternatively, you may just pin it at this time.

9. For the burlap or linen pine trees and stars you need an extra step because these materials ravel unless glue or fray check is used on the edges. I do not recommend using the plastic sheet bonding material for these. Instead, lay down a piece of waxed paper, place the shape, front side down, on it and then run a thin line of glue or fray check around the edges. Next, take a disposable fine paint brush and brush the glue/fray check all the way out to the edges to capture every fiber that could possibly ravel off. While the glue/fray check is still wet, place the pine tree or star back on the pennant where you want it, press it firmly, especially around the edges, and allow to dry.

10. Once you have all of the shapes pinned or adhered to the pennants, use a simple running or blanket stitch to sew them down. Use your silver/gray perle cotton or embroidery floss for this. Remove pins when finished stitching.

11. Now, fold the pennants over so that the exterior (right) sides are out. Pin around the outer edge to hold the two sides of the pennants neatly in place. Using your

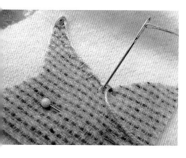

worsted weight wool, use a running or blanket stitch to decoratively sew the edges together, leaving enough open at the top end (not the pointy end) to run your cording through.

12. Once you have finished all six pennants, string them on your cording or ribbon, leaving a small space between each pennant. Secure each pennant from sliding along the cording by adding a small tack stitch with your worsted yarn on either side of the pennant through the cording. You may choose to knot the ends of the cording or make hanging loops.

Your garland is now ready to hang in a doorway, over a Christmas tree, on a mantel, or wherever you think it looks best to bring some winter cheer to your home!

Needle-Felted Maine Balsam Sachets

We are so spoiled in Maine to be surrounded by fragrant balsam fir year-round. When I was a child living in New Jersey, one of the things I loved about coming to Maine was the fresh, bracing scent of the pine and balsam. I loved the balsam fir sachets that were everywhere in the tourist shops at that time. To this day, when I've been away from Maine somewhere to our south and am coming back home via the Maine Turnpike, I almost always stop at the Maine welcome center at Kittery, whether I think I need a driving break or not. Why? Because as soon as you open the car door at that rest area, the scent of Maine pine/balsam greets you. That is my "welcome home" from every trip south.

Maine balsam sachets can still be purchased all across the state as souvenirs, in both quirky small independent gift shops as well as at international retailer, LL Bean. However,

it is so very easy to make your own and doing so gives you the chance to personalize the sachet for desired size and style. They make particularly good holiday gifts or stocking stuffers because many people associate the fragrance of balsam with the holiday season.

These sachets can be used to freshen drawers and closets, as pin cushions, as a restful scent for under your pillow at night, or as a calming object to keep in your desk or purse as needed. Much like lavender, the scent of balsam is comforting to many people and helps with stress management.

In this project, we are making a 4" x 4" wool balsam sachet with a decorative needle felted design on it, but you could use any fabric you like or have on hand for a simpler, non-needle felted project. Balsam fir sachets are a great way to repurpose fabrics. You can make your sachets extra meaningful by perhaps using the shirt of a loved one, a special baby blanket that is worn beyond use, a piece of a wedding dress that would be otherwise discarded, or anything that has a place in your heart. Small sachets also make great wedding or party favors, giving guests something beautiful and useful to take home.

While it is possible to make your own balsam stuffing from an expired Christmas tree or holiday wreath, I get my balsam very fresh from Maine Balsam Fir company in nearby West Paris, Maine. The reason I buy it vs making it myself is because I have found that the proprietary natural process used by Maine Balsam Fir results in a more fragrant, consistent, and lasting product. I buy it in bulk for the many hooked balsam pillows I make for my business, but you can purchase it in a variety of smaller package sizes. Maine Balsam Fir ships all over the world, sending a little bit of Maine to every customer. Lucky for me, I just take a ten-minute drive to their retail shop and processing facility to purchase mine.

NOTE: If you truly want to harvest your own balsam, simply strip the short needles off of your fir wreaths or Christmas trees at the end of the season, removing any small stems or branches. It is neatest to do this outside, perhaps spreading an old blanket or sheet underneath the wreath or tree. Take the small needles and store them in a paper bag or even a pillowcase. These will be fragrant too and are perfectly serviceable.

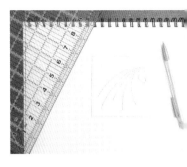

You Will Need

Wool for the outer sachet cover, 4.5" x 9"
Design or pattern for the outer sachet cover
Sharpie
Red dot or other pattern transfer material
Straight pins
Wool roving in a variety of colors for felting your design
One or two needle felting needles, one coarse, one fine
Needle felting block
Yarn for whip stitch finishing, about 2 yards
Tapestry needle
Cotton muslin for the sachet interiors, 4.5" x 9"
Quilting square or ruler
Sewing machine or hand needle and thread
Fresh Maine balsam, about 1 cup
Measuring cup
Wide mouth canning funnel

Instructions for the Felted Sachet Exterior

For this decorative balsam sachet, I used a very simple white pine needle design. You may use that also or you may want to draw your own design. The instructions for transferring the design on the wool surface will be the same either way.

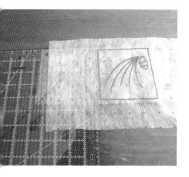

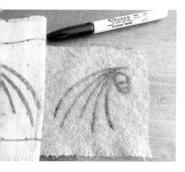

1. For a 4" x 4" sachet, cut your exterior wool piece 4.5" x 9" to leave a little allowance for the whipstitch edge finish at the end. This project does not rely on precision, so don't stress too much about exact measurements but do get close.

2. Use your Sharpie to lightly mark the center line that bisects the 9" dimension. In other words, if you fold your wool in half along that line, you will have a 4.5" x 4.5" square. This light marking will be on the interior of the sachet but will serve as a guideline for centering your design.

3. Place your red dot or other transfer material over the design template provided (or your own appropriately sized design). Using your Sharpie, trace the design on to the transfer material.

4. Carefully place the marked transfer material on to the surface of your outer sachet wool, being careful that the bisecting line is on the interior side and that you're going to put the design on the exterior side.

5. Using that bisecting line as a guide, center the design on the transfer material on to the half of the wool that will be the front of your sachet (you may pin it in place if you like) and Sharpie over it so that the ink bleeds through on to the wool.

6. Remove the transfer material. If the design lines on the wool are too faint to work with, simply go over them again, either with or without the transfer material, to make them more visible.

7. Now place your wool with the design on it on to your foam felting block. If you would like to, you can pin it in place on the block by just inserting straight pins at the corners directly down into the foam.

8. Begin needle felting! You will be amazed at how easy and fun this is. Choose your first color of roving to work with. I chose to begin with the forest green and felt the

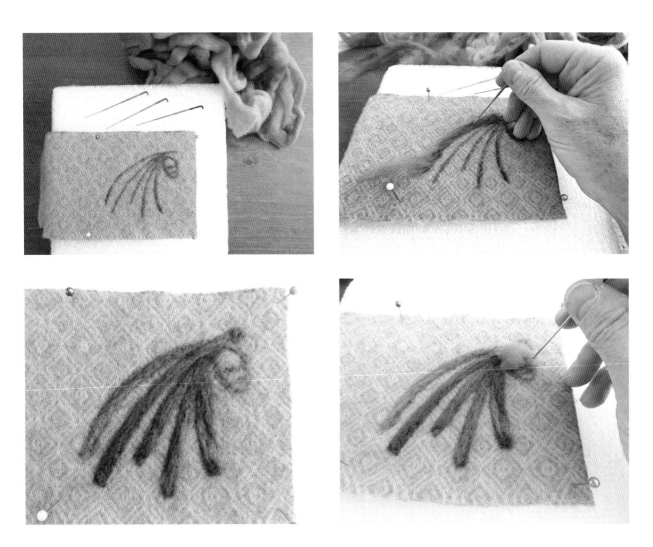

needles on first. Take small pieces of roving, pulling off maybe an inch or two of a thin strip at a time, lay it on to your design line, and start stabbing quickly at it with the coarser needle. The roving will immediately start to adhere to the wool wherever you stab it down. Continue stabbing the roving down and along the pine needle lines until you have completely covered the Sharpie lines with the roving.

9. You may refine the lines with the finer needle by shaping them, again with a stabbing motion, along their edges to make cleaner lines.

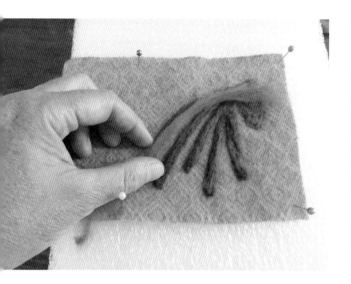
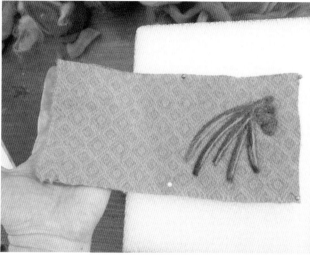

10. You may now want to layer on some rust browns and a lighter green as a highlight color. Take small pieces of your highlight colors and begin stabbing them in to place along the edges of the dark green pine needles. It need not be a solid highlight line. You may wish to just accentuate the curve of the needles or skip some needles altogether. This is a very intuitive and subjective process and it is impossible to do it wrong.

11. Next, I used the rust colored roving to create the small pinecone at the top of the needle bunch. These can also be shaded with a darker rust, and you can layer in additional roving to create height and texture.

12. Keep adding small pieces of roving, in your desired colors, to the design until a) all of the black pattern markings are hidden and b) you feel satisfied that your design is finished

13. When you feel that your design is all finished, unpin your wool and gently lift it from the felting block. It may feel like it has slightly adhered to the block. This is normal. Set this aside and go on to creating the balsam insert for your sachet.

Instructions for the Balsam Sachet Insert

This insert will go inside your 4" x 4" exterior sachet cover.
For sachets, I always use a pillow insert that is at least the
size of the exterior, not smaller. This creates a fluffy finished
sachet which is especially important with balsam because
balsam can contract a little over time. Therefore, you will
make your piece of muslin 4.5" x 9" for a finished insert that
will measure, with seam allowance, just about 4" x 4" when
completed.

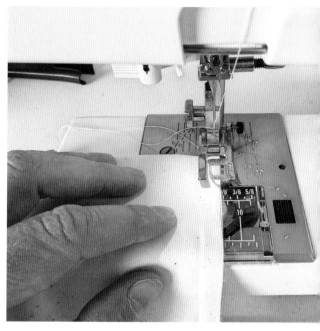

1. Using your quilting square or very carefully with a ruler, making sure your corners are truly ninety degrees, measure out your muslin and mark your cutting lines with a pencil. Again, your dimensions for this piece of muslin are 4.5" x 9".

2. Fold the muslin in half so that you have a square measuring 4.5" x 4.5". Pin in place leaving plenty of room for your machine sewn seam.

3. Sew two sides shut, leaving about 1/8 to 1/4 inch for the seam.

4. Turn your insert right side out now. Gently poke the corners completely out from the inside with the tip of your scissors.

5. Pop your canning funnel into the open end of the insert and using a small measuring cup fill the insert with

balsam. Do not be afraid to really stuff it almost all the way to the top, leaving about ¾ of an inch so that you can still comfortably pin it shut to sew the final seam. I find this size insert will take about a cup of balsam.

6. Breathe in the scent of the balsam. You may repeat this step as many times as you like. It's tempting to call this optional, but really, why would we want to make this optional?

7. Carefully pin all the way across the top opening in such a way that it will hold all the balsam back while you sew the final closing seam.

8. Machine or hand sew the last seam. If you are very concerned with neatness you may fold the seam allowance back and then sew. Typically, I consider these inserts utilitarian and invisible in the final project and do not bother to fold back the edges prior to sewing.

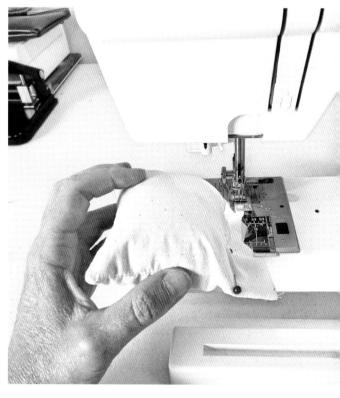

NOTE: If you have one, a serger or overlock machine makes very quick work of sewing inserts. The closing seam especially is zipped neatly shut with all excess fabric cut away in one expedient operation by the serger/overlock blade.

Finishing the Sachet

Now it's time to finish the sachet! We are using an easy technique called yarn whip stitching to bind the edges of the wool sachet exterior together. This is quick and simple; however, you could also choose to use a blanket stitch or any other decorative stitch you know to close your sachet.

1. Thread your color coordinating yarn through your tapestry needle, using a piece about 18" to 24" long. Make a small knot at the end of the yarn and cut off the excess. If you find as you stitch that your yarn is starting to wind up on itself, simply drop the needle, let the yarn unwind, and resume sewing.

2. Fold your wool exterior in half and pin the sides evenly, right side facing out. This is not a technique where you sew the piece on the wrong side and then flip it right side out. Rather, it is a decorative edging applied to the exterior, right side of the piece.

3. Remember that you need to leave one side open to stuff the exterior with your balsam interior sachet.

4. Starting near a corner, push the tapestry needle through an inside edge of the cover so that the knot in the yarn will hide on the interior. Then, using an overhand whip stitch, start stitching around and around the very edge of the sachet, placing each stitch next to the one before it. Make the stitches about an ⅛ inch to no more than a ¼ inch on the edges. Making the stitches too wide will impact your ability to stuff the pillow with your 4" x 4" balsam insert.

5. When you go around corners, you may have to use some extra stitches to fully cover the corner. Work around the corners intuitively, manually adjusting the stitches if necessary, to completely cover the wool edge.

6. When you reach the point where you have just one open side, place the balsam insert inside the pillow and resume stitching.

OPTIONAL: For the side of the sachet that is the fold in the wool, you may leave it as is, with three sides of the pillow whip stitched (I think this gives it a little extra out-of-the-box character), or you may continue whip stitching that side too. It's a faux seam but adds balance to the other three if that's what you prefer.

That's it! Your sachet is fragrant and finished! This project is so quick and simple, but yields such a quality result, that it makes an ideal winter's day project. The sachets also make nice hostess or teacher's gifts and stocking stuffers.

Heritage Skills for Contemporary Living

Winter Recipes

Parris House New England Clam Chowder—A Nontraditional Take

When I moved to Maine in 2000, I wanted to learn everything the Maine or New England way. I wanted to know how to make regional recipes the "right" way and to embrace traditions in the most authentic ways I could. I even bought and have treasured Maine author Marjorie Standish's book, *Keep Cooking – The Maine Way,* as an introduction to recipes native to the area. This was fun for a while and I learned a lot. It also made me feel more at home in my new surroundings and helped me feel a little less "from away," although let me tell you, having not been born in Maine I will always be from away. So, I learned to make New England clam chowder from a variety of traditional recipes, however, as time went on, I started to add my own modifications, some influenced by my Italian heritage. Some of my friends have asked for the recipe. Others have good naturedly declared the chowder a blasphemy against New England.

Deciding to include this recipe in a book created a conundrum for me. I don't use recipes for many of my soups. Soups are a thing that evolve in my kitchen, as the spirit and the ingredients on hand move me. As a result, I have written here my best approximation of how this soup is made (and I did test the recipe, rest assured) even though on a typical snowy afternoon, it's going together in a more unstructured way. I hope you enjoy it and I think some of you will recognize the ingredients that many native Mainers would say "don't belong." There is also a traditional ingredient missing.

Prep time: **30 minutes**

Cook time: **20 minutes**

Serves: **12**

Ingredients

1 10-ounce can clams in juices
1 12-ounce package frozen clams
1 8-ounce bottle clam juice
32 ounces vegetable broth
1/2 stick (1/8 pound) butter
1 large onion
6 medium to large potatoes, diced in to
   1 inch pieces, peeling is optional
4 cups whole milk
2 cups half and half
1 teaspoon minced garlic
1 teaspoon dried rosemary
Salt and pepper to taste
4 cups fresh kale or green of your choice chopped

Directions

1. Reserving the juice, thaw and drain the frozen clams and drain the canned clams. Set juice aside. Keep clams cold until use.
2. In a heavy stock pot or Dutch oven melt the butter over medium heat.
3. Sauté the onions and garlic in the butter until slightly soft.
4. Add the diced potatoes and toss them around to get them coated in the butter.
5. Add the vegetable stock and the drained and bottled clam juice and simmer, covered, over low heat until the potatoes are fork tender.
6. Keep the heat low to avoid scorching on the bottom and add the milk and half and half. Bring the entire mixture back up to a point where it is hot, but not boiling.
7. Add the rosemary, salt, and pepper to taste.

8. Add the clams. Do not boil them in the soup, lest they become tough and rubbery, plus boiling will cause the dairy in the soup to foam. Just simmer on a low heat for about ten minutes.

9. There are two ways to use your chopped greens in this soup. One, you can drop the chopped greens in to the soup, stir lightly to evenly distribute them, and then put the lid on for about five minutes letting the greens lightly cook in the soup. Alternatively, you can simply put your greens in the bottom of your soup bowl when serving and ladle the soup on top of it, allowing them to wilt in the hot soup as it is eaten. It just depends on how tender or crisp you want the greens to be and how much you want the taste of the greens to subsequently permeate the soup.

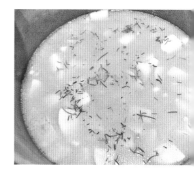

OPTIONS:

- If you make your own yogurt or cheese, you may have liquid whey in the house. If you do, you can substitute some or all of the vegetable broth with the whey for a tangier flavor and a protein boost.

- Also, if you like your chowder thick, add corn starch, a tablespoon at a time, mixed well with just enough cold water for it to dissolve, in to the hot chowder until the desired thickness is attained. Again, do not overheat or bring to a rolling boil as this may make the clams tough. The corn starch will thicken the soup even if it is not boiling.

This chowder is especially nice served with a crusty home-made bread, possibly with a roasted garlic spread. As with most homemade soups and chowders, it also tastes better the second or even the third day when the flavors have all had a chance to further coalesce. Be gentle when warming it up the next day, again to protect the flavor and texture of the clams.

Honey Pumpkin Bread with Roasted Pumpkin Seeds

Prep time: **30 minutes**

Bake time: **55 minutes**

Serves: **8**

I love fresh pumpkin, so much so that I often just cook it, mash it, and eat it with a little bit of salt and butter. If you pureed and froze your fall pumpkins well, you will find that they taste just about as good as when they were fresh and can be used for soups, pies, cakes, and this bread. If you don't have pumpkin puree put up in your freezer, you can use canned. This is not a super sweet bread where the pumpkin flavor is lost behind sugar. Instead it has about the sweetness level of traditional New England brown bread. However, if you find it not quite sweet enough for your tastes, add ½ cup sugar in your next batch or spread apple butter or another sweet preserve on it.

Ingredients

2 cups self-rising flour

15 ounces pumpkin puree

4 eggs

½ cup honey

2 tablespoons molasses

3 tablespoons butter, melted

½ teaspoon cinnamon

¼ teaspoon cloves

¼ teaspoon ground ginger

3 tablespoons roasted pumpkin seeds coated with honey

OPTIONAL: You may substitute a teaspoon of pumpkin pie spice for the spices listed here.

To Make Honeyed Pumpkin Seeds

1. Heat oven to 400 degrees
2. Coat an iron skillet with vegetable oil
3. Spread out the pumpkin seeds in the bottom of the pan
4. Roast for 5 minutes in hot oven or until crispy but not overly browned
5. Remove from oven and allow to cool until they are just warm to the touch
6. Using a spoon coat the seeds in about a teaspoon of honey until evenly covered
Set aside

To Make the Bread

1. Reduce oven temperature to 350 degrees

2. Grease and flour a 5" x 9" loaf pan

3. Combine the pumpkin puree, eggs, honey, molasses, and spices in your mixer bowl and combine until the eggs are broken and mixed in

4. Add the melted butter once it is cooled enough not to "cook" the eggs in the batter, mix until smooth

5. Add the self-rising flour one cup at a time and beat until you have a smooth batter

6. Turn the batter evenly in to the prepared pan Sprinkle the honey coated seeds evenly on top of the loaf

7. Bake 40 – 50 minutes or until a knife poked into the center comes out clean

8. Remove from oven when done and allow to cool for at least half an hour before turning the bread out from the pan and slicing.

Heritage Skills for Contemporary Living

Wood Stove or Oven-Roasted Fall/ Winter Vegetables in Cast Iron

This recipe is a chance to let your lovingly grown, tended, and preserved garden harvest shine. Roasting fall/winter vegetables over a steady heat in cast iron brings out their flavor in an unparalleled way. While I'm going to be using vegetables that I grew and grow regularly in this recipe, you may substitute your own as long as they are firm fleshed (like winter squash vs summer squash, which would be a bit soft for this recipe) and you find the flavors pleasing in combination. This is simple, incredibly nutritious, and soul satisfying winter fare.

We have a medium sized wood fired heating stove in the Parris House kitchen, the top of which we use in winter for roasting vegetables, simmering soups, heating water, and more. We do not really have the space or layout to have a large wood fired cook stove, but if you do, by all means use it. I am such a believer in wood fired cooking that if we had the space for a full cook stove, we'd absolutely have one. If you do not have a wood fired stove of any kind, this recipe will work just fine in a conventional oven set to around 375 degrees F.

If you do not have cast iron skillets and are using a conventional oven, a heavy ceramic baking dish will also do, however, do not use your ceramic baking dish on top of a wood stove. Having said that, although my intent is never to have you go out and buy anything you don't need, I do believe that owning at least one good sized (10" or 12") cast iron skillet changes your cooking life, for the better, forever. At the Parris House we have about six in a variety of sizes and use them almost daily.

The advantages of cast iron are many. For one thing, with good care, cast iron cookware is forever. You can easily find perfectly serviceable cast iron that is a century old and I

Prep time: **15 minutes**

Cook time: **60 minutes**

Serves: **6 – 8**

fully intend to pass my cast iron down to the next generation of family.

There are many schools of thought and so-called rules for taking care of your cast iron cookware. Some say "never use soap on cast iron." I personally do not subscribe to this. As someone who cooks anything and everything in cast iron, including fish and dishes with lots and lots of garlic, there are times when I want the assistance of a mild dish detergent to really clean the pan and eliminate any lingering odors. If the pan is used frequently and has become well-seasoned, soap will not ruin the seasoning, or non-stick properties of the pan. I do not, however, allow water to stand in my cast iron cookware for very long and once I have cleaned it, I set it either on a hot wood stove or put it over the gas flame on my range to dry very quickly. This prevents rust. If you are not using your cast iron cookware every day, it's a good idea to wipe it down with a thin layer of vegetable oil to further prevent oxidation, but I use my cast iron so frequently that I often skip this step.

Most new cast iron cookware is seasoned right out of the box, but if you're inheriting or buying vintage cookware, just pay attention to whether food is sticking to it or if it seems to rust very easily. If those things are happening, just coat it with a thin layer of oil and put it in a very hot oven (450 degrees or higher) for several hours. Turn the oven off and allow the pan to cool. Test it again and you should get much better results.

As you can tell, I do not believe in making a big deal out of babying cast iron cookware, especially for every day home use. This is a type of cookware that has been with us for hundreds of years, was used to cook meals under harsh and inconvenient conditions for our Revolutionary and Civil War soldiers, is found at modern campsites today (although not so much with backpack campers; a little heavy for that!), and in every possible kitchen situation including open hearth cooking. It will most certainly perform admirably in your modern kitchen using every day cooking and cleaning methods.

Another advantage of cast iron is that once it's hot, it's hot and does not cool down quickly. Contrary to popular belief, cast iron does not heat up evenly because it is a poor conductor of heat. In fact, it's possible to get hot spots on a cast iron pan as it's heating on a stovetop. If you really need to avoid this (e.g. you want to sear a steak), put the pan in the oven to get it hot before putting it on your stove burner. However, cast iron does hold and radiate heat like a champ. Consider how a cast iron wood stove literally works by holding and radiating heat efficiently. This makes cast iron cookware an excellent choice for roasting vegetables, roasting whole chicken or pot roast, or even baking bread. Additionally, any food that is in direct contact with the cast iron pan bottom or sides will brown nicely or form a crust, which is especially delectable in a roast vegetable dish, which, I realize is the recipe you started reading this for.

Ingredients

6 cups winter squash, cut into about 1-inch cubes
4 cups carrots (the more colorful, the better), sliced into chunky rounds
2 cup parsnips, sliced into chunky rounds
1 coarsely cubed apple (optional), peeled or not, depending on taste
3 cloves garlic, sliced
1 teaspoon yellow curry powder
½ teaspoon ground ginger (or, if you like more snap, add small chunks of fresh ginger)
¼ teaspoon white or black pepper
Salt to taste
4 tablespoons olive oil
Fresh parsley, basil, or cilantro for garnish.

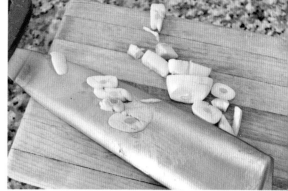

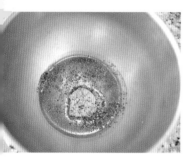

Directions

1. If oven baking, preheat oven to 375 degrees F.
2. Peel the vegetables and cut off the ends, saving the vegetable scraps for your chickens, other livestock, or compost pile.
3. Smack the garlic cloves hard with the palm of your hand over the flat side of a large chopping knife (do not have any skin near the knife's blade edge!), then peel, and chop in to coarse pieces.
4. Place the vegetables and garlic in to a large mixing bowl and set aside.
5. In a small mixing bowl, mix 3 tablespoons of the olive oil and all of the seasonings except the end garnish.
6. Use 1 tablespoon of olive oil to oil the iron skillet, bottom and sides.
7. Pour the olive oil and seasoning mixture over the vegetables and toss to coat evenly.
8. Transfer the coated vegetables to a 10-inch or larger iron skillet. Spread the vegetables evenly in the pan.
9. Cover with a fitted lid or aluminum foil.
10. If cooking on top of a wood stove, be sure to turn the vegetables frequently with a metal spatula to keep them from browning too much on the bottom. Add a little oil a bit at a time if you find that there's any sticking at all.
11. If baking in the oven, check and turn occasionally to also achieve even browning of the vegetables.
12. If you are adding the apple as an optional ingredient,

wait until the vegetables are about three quarters of the way cooked, then gently mix in the apples so that they are still somewhat firm when the vegetables are finished.

13. The vegetables are done when they are fork-tender, 45 to 60 minutes.

14. Garnish with fresh parsley, basil, or cilantro before serving.

NOTE: There are several ways to tell approximately how hot the cook plate is on your wood stove, but my favorite is a modern infrared thermometer which can be pointed at the hot plate and will give back an accurate enough reading to be useful. Cooking on a wood stove cook plate is not an exact science, and watching your dish as it cooks, turning the contents if they are browning too quickly, adjusting the stove down if you are concerned about burning, are all things that become more and more intuitive over time. However, having a quick gauge of cook plate temperature is one more helpful bit of information as you learn to cook on your wood stove.

EPILOGUE

NOW IT'S YOUR TURN

I wanted to write this book because I believe in a philosophy of creation. I believe that all of us are born with an innate desire to create and that, especially in modern times, we limit the definition of creativity. Our senses are flooded daily with external definitions of creativity through social media, television, and most insidious of all, advertising. Most of what we are exposed to through those media are definitions of creativity with an agenda. That agenda is not to encourage you to plumb the depths of your own inherent creativeness. It is usually about selling you someone else's definition of what's creative. Ironically, while media and advertising are branding "authenticity," they are at the same time attempting to influence and shape your sense of taste. That's not where your best way of living comes from.

You are authentic. Your interests, your creativity, and your tastes are authentic and the act of making or creating helps you discover your own areas of creative interest. I hope, with this book, you have discovered not only a new skill, but something new about yourself. In the nearly twenty years we've lived at the Parris House I've discovered that I love growing my own food. I now know that I love making more rustic, hearty family style meals and that delicate souffles or painstakingly made chocolate roses are not going to be a common thing in my cooking repertoire. I know that wool is my medium of choice, that I have a passion for everything about it: its texture, its versatility, even its smell. Best of all, I've learned that as a teacher my favorite students are beginners. I love being present for discovery, for that moment when students who thought they weren't talented, weren't creative, weren't at all like the influencer they follow, suddenly discover that maybe they are, that maybe none of this is that mysterious.

So, now it's your turn. It's your turn to discover what you love to do and what fits your lifestyle. I offer the following thoughts on how to continue from here:

Get creative with friends and family. Instead of inviting people over for dinner, invite them over to make dinner together. Create a shared garden or apiary instead of just having one on your own. Start a crafting group and get together on a regular basis.

Look for classes in your area. Continuing or adult education programs within your local school district are a great resource for everything from soap making to fiber art to beekeeping. There are often classes offered through university cooperative extensions, community colleges, and local art and craft studios as well.

Go to makers' fairs and farmers' markets and ask questions. Makers and growers usually love to talk about what they do. Ask them about their processes, their materials, how they learned, and ask them to give you a demonstration. If someone is secretive about what they do, they are not helping to perpetuate their art or skill for future generations.

Support local small farmers and businesses. When you support your local producers and artisans you are helping to sustain the availability of not only their products, but their practice and ability to pass on knowledge.

Talk to the older folks. Some of the older generation today were among the first who went all out embracing modern convenience living, but find the ones who kept some of the old-time ways and ask them for their stories. Did their mothers make their clothes for them and what do they remember about that? Is there a favorite family recipe that involves a gardening or cooking skill that you could learn? Does someone have a hooked rug that is decades old and could be repaired or reproduced if someone just showed the interest?

Talk to the young people. There is a very tangible resurgence in interest in heritage skills among the young. Pay careful attention to what interests them and learn from it. If you immerse yourself in the creative and homesteading communities you will find many young people, couples, and whole families adopting a more DIY lifestyle. Sometimes this is borne of a desire to engage in more socially and environmentally sustainable ways of living and sometimes too it is borne of necessity. Some heritage skills are money saving, which is a plus for people just starting out in life.

Involve the kids. If you have children or grandchildren, pass down what you know. You can help keep kids from becoming disconnected with their environment and falling into a consumerist lifestyle by teaching them to interact with the planet and make things on their own.

Think back to your own childhood. Was there a particular art class you remember lighting up over? Was there something a family member did that you wanted to try too? Were you involved in an art or skill in high school or college that you let fall away as you went on to "real life?" I was involved in many arts when I was growing up. I played several instruments, wrote, did limited needle work, and dabbled in pastel art. For a lot of reasons, when I went to college to study Business Administration, all of that was put on hold, for a couple of decades, as it turned out. Look back at what you enjoyed in your youth and see if there's anything you'd like to pick up again. This is how my husband re-entered the world of ceramics.

Find mentors who not only know how to do the things you want to learn, but who are simpatico with who you are. I cannot emphasize this enough. A truly great mentor clicks with your personality, your goals, and cheers you on well into your own achievement of competency and expertise. Good mentors want to see you succeed and take joy in seeing one more person carrying the knowledge into the future.

Be fearless. If there's one thing I hope you've taken from this book, it's that nothing is rocket science. I worked with rocket scientists at that defense company that employed me in my former life. Even for them, the work was just learning their vocation one step at a time. The stakes are much lower in making and homesteading. If you make a mistake, the consequences are relatively, well . . . inconsequential. I think our worst failures involved losing bee colonies over the winter. Because we were working with living things, we felt those losses deeply and felt the responsibility for them. It's a rare beekeeper, though, who has not lost a colony, especially in their early years of beekeeping. If your failure involves a recipe or a piece of art or craft, the results may be disappointing, or even cost you some money, but are not of great long-term consequence. The lesson in that is, learn from your mistakes and keep going.

It has been an adventure for me to write this book. This is my first book, so in writing it I had a bit of the learning curve experience you may be having in trying the recipes and projects it contains. I hope you have learned something new, can use the contents as an ongoing reference, and will even consider visiting us here at the Parris House someday. If you do, we know we will, in turn, learn something from your story and your experience. Until then, enjoy your new skills and pass them on.

RESOURCES

History

Paris Hill Historical Society
48 Tremont Street, Paris, Maine 04271
facebook.com/parishillhistoricalsociety

Hamlin Memorial Library and Museum
16 Hannibal Hamlin Drive, Paris, Maine
04271
facebook.com/hamlinlibrary

Paris Cape Historical Society
19 Park Street, South Paris, Maine 04281
facebook.com/
ParisCapeHistoricalSociety

Historic New England
141 Cambridge Street
Boston, MA 02114
historicnewengland.org

Gardening/Preserving

Paris Farmers Union
parisfarmersunion.com

Aubuchon Hardware
hardwarestore.com

Tractor Supply
tractorsupply.com

Pinetree Garden Seeds
superseeds.com

Johnny's Selected Seeds
johnnyseeds.com

University of Maine Cooperative Extension
extension.umaine.edu

Post Carbon Designs
postcarbondesigns.com

Kilner
kilnerjar.co.uk

Ball Canning
freshpreserving.com

Beekeeping

Backwoods Bee Farm
106 Page Road, Windham, Maine 04062
backwoodsbeefarm.com

Better Bee
betterbee.com

Maine State Beekeepers Association
mainebeekeepers.org

Maine State Apiary Program
maine.gov/dacf/php/apiary/index.shtml

Rug Hooking/Fiber Art

Parris House Wool Works
546 Paris Hill Road, Paris, Maine 04281
parrishousewoolworks.com (use password
HeritageSkills to access pdf files of pattern
templates)

Two Cats and Dog Hooking
twocatsanddoghooking.com

Deanne Fitzpatrick Studio
hookingrugs.com

Encompassing Designs Rug Hooking Studio
encompassingdesigns.com

Susan Feller, ArtWools
artwools.com

Dorr Mill Store
dorrmillstore.com

Cushing Dyes
wcushing.com/product/
perfection-acid-dyes

Magic Carpet Dyes
wandaworks.ca/store/c2/Majic_Carpet_
Dyes.html

Greener Shades
greenershades.com

Jacquard Dyes
jacquardproducts.com/acid-dye

Pro Chemical and Dye
prochemicalanddye.net

The International Guild of Handhooking
Rugmakers (TIGHR)
prochemicalanddye.net

Association of Traditional Hooking Artists
(ATHA)
atharugs.com
Beeline Art Tools (wool cutters)
beelinearttools.com

Sizzix (wool cutters)
theoldtatteredflag.com/Sizzix-Wool-
Cutting-Package-Cut-60-Strips-with-1-
Turn-2245.html

Rug Hooking Magazine
rughookingmagazine.com
Fiber Trends (felting supplies)
fibertrends.com

Fiber & Vine (yarns, felting supplies, knitting patterns, & more)
402 Main Street, Norway, Maine 04268
fiberandvine.com

Wool is Why (hand dyed roving and fiber)
facebook.com/WoolIsWhy

Sue Spargo (hand stitching, quilting, & more)
suespargo.com/index.php

Making Magazine
makingzine.com

Maine Balsam Fir (balsam for pillow
interiors)
mainebalsam.com

Life Experiences, Inc (buckwheat seeds &
hulls for pillow interiors)
buckwheathull.com

207 Creatives (annual windjammer hooking
trip aboard the Schooner J&E Riggin)
facebook.com/207creatives

Soap Making

Brambleberry (soap and beeswax pellets)
brambleberry.com

Soap Queen
soapqueen.com

Chicken Keeping

Lisa Steele, Fresh Eggs Daily
fresheggsdaily.com

Meyer Hatchery
meyerhatchery.com

ACKNOWLEDGMENTS

As I've mentioned, this is my first book and I owe so much to so many for helping me navigate this project. I am a Type A person who was fortunately and serendipitously matched with editor Michael Steere at Down East Books, who was calm, capable, and collected at all times. So, I'd like to thank Michael for his expertise, patience, and guidance through this process. I'd also like to thank my Retail and Production Manager at Parris House Wool Works, Heather Daggett, for sitting down and helping me proof this manuscript, page by page, image by image. And, of course, I'd like to thank Down East Books and Rowman & Littlefield for saying "yes" to a first book in a niche genre.

Over the past twenty years I have had such good mentoring and guidance in learning the skills I've shared in this book. Among those who have been invaluable fiber art teachers or simply inspirations in the art are Connie Fletcher of Seven Gables Rug Hooking, Susan Feller of ArtWools, Christine Little of Encompassing Designs, Karen Miller, Deanne Fitzpatrick, Meryl Cook, Mary DeLano, Kim Hamlin of Fiber & Vine, and my partner in 207 Creatives, Ellen Marshall of Two Cats & Dog Hooking.

I owe much of what I know about chicken keeping to Lisa Steele of Fresh Eggs Daily, who not only is always up for a poultry question, but was incredibly generous with her knowledge of writing and publishing when I first set out to send proposals for this book to publishers. I have to tell you, though, Lisa's coop will always be cuter than mine.

Beekeeping is a complex and confusing pursuit, made quite a bit less so by my beekeeping teacher, Carol Cottrill, mentors Vanessa & Chris Rogers of Backwoods Bee Farm in Windham, Maine and by my original mentor, Eric Davis. Vanessa talked me through my first swarm and is always there to walk me back from the ledge when something goes wrong. Best of all, she's also a gifted rug hooker.

I am lucky to have so many historical resources right here in Paris and around our state and region. I'd like to thank the Paris Hill Historical Society for the use of their archives for both general information and for access to the diaries of Arabella Rawson Carter. I'd also like to thank Historic New England for the use of images relating to Pedro Tovookan Parris. The foremost expert on the life of Tovookan remains Dr. Martha McNamara of Wellesley College who is currently writing Tovookan's biography and who has given generously of this knowledge to me and to the Paris Hill community.

I owe my knowledge of photographing projects and writing their instructions to my work as a contributor to both *Making Magazine* and *Rug Hooking Magazine* where experienced editors first walked me through those processes. Because of their previous guidance, I felt more confident in writing the project sections in this book.

Companies and venues who have partnered with me for retailing and teaching have helped introduce my work to a wider audience. These creative partners include Dr. Brent Ridge and Josh Kilmer-Purcell of Beekman 1802, Sabbathday Lake Shaker Village, Squam Art Workshops, Portfiber, Fiber & Vine, Stitchery in Rhode Island, Oxford Mill End Store, and Darn Good Yarn. Additionally, we have creative partners who make products for sale through Parris House Wool Works. These include Ron Adams of Bear Pond Wood Works, Edna Olmstead, Carolyn Homa, Pat Hutter, and my husband, Bill, of Sunset Haven Pottery. I am grateful for all of these.

None of my work would be possible without the ongoing support of the friends and customers of Parris House Wool Works, both online and in person, including those who join us for our weekly Tuesday hooking group. Since our operations are based right out of the Parris House in our National Historic District, I am also grateful to my neighbors in the Paris Hill community for accepting and supporting my homestead and studio.

Most importantly, I owe everything to my family. My husband, Bill, has been an unwavering supporter of my small enterprise, gently and not-so-gently pushing me to continue on days I've thought seriously about giving up. My four sons and my niece grew up helping me with my homesteading experiments and witnessing both my successes and failures. They are also directly responsible for teaching me some of the skills contained in this book. They are Robert Miller, his wife, Tracy Miller, and their son, Oliver, James Miller and his wife, Beth Fancy, Peter Miller, Paul Miller and his fiancée Gabriela Rabasa, and my niece, Rose Colangelo and her boyfriend, Oscar Nemeth.